Becoming What You Need

Practices For Embodying Nonviolent Communication

David K. Weinstock

Dedication

For my wife Judith who's embodiment of what I have endeavored
so long to articulate has been my guiding light and to my
family and community who make it all worth while.

Gratitude and Acknowledgements

Copious gratitude to John Pierce for all his editing and generous guidance: to Louise Jacobsen for her insights, encouragement, and attention to detail, to Robert Dash's photographic prowess and helpful hints, to Xio Lugo for gracing this cover and overall book design with her artistry, to the teachers that I have been fortunate to have at my back –Sensei Koichi Barrish, Dr. Richard Strozzi, Wendy Palmer, Dr. Stuart Heller, Dr. Marshal Rosenberg, and Norman Wachler. To all the NVC, Aikido and Somatic teachers and practitioners who have inspired me along the way. To friends, family and associates for their suggestions, guidance and serious conversations – Karen Sella, David Smith, David and Fran Korton, Kathy Kelly, Wendy Garrido, Paul Linden, Bill Leicht, James Nybo, Lucy Leu, Debbie Hindmen, Punita Greenberg, John Hazlett, Robyn Caywood, Crista Bock, Paul Bartick, Shelley, Jack, Judith, Sharon, Devin, Sam, and so many more.

Praise for Somatic Consensus

and Practices For Embodying Nonviolent Communication

"A great way to have hope about the most heated and wounded relationship."

~ Kathy Buys, Psychologist

"David's work is a labor of love and a gift to all those fortunate enough to experience it. Somatic Consensus's collaborative, experiential teachings encourage subtle reflection on core behavioral patterns, and more skillful expressions of centered, compassionate ways of being in the world."

~ Karen Sella, Luminere Somatics

"These are seeds planted in my body that I believe will keep sprouting. It's the practice of feeling Nonviolent Communication distinctions in the body–that's where the integration occurs!"

~ Kirsten Elfandahl, Executive Director of Freedom Project

"This work is a direct way into cultivating the intrinsic trust I've been seeking. This unified somatic internal consensus among body, mind, and spirit that David has been honing is NVC in motion. It has opened up a piece of the empathic field that has been out of my reach."

~ Shana Deane, International Institute for Restorative Practices

"Here you'll find a coherent approach to NVC through your body and perceptions. You'll discover you have unsuspected and unused strengths in your own body."

~ Bill Leicht, President of Urban Visions

"These practices are a great way to help individuals in a community process deepen into their own sense of personal meaning and strength for the benefit of the whole."

~ Chloe Brown, College Student

"This work cultivates a deep awareness of embodied habits and exciting new skills to help you return to center, stay neutral in crisis, and lead with your heart."

~ Jane Falkner, Psychotherapist

"I want to tell you that hardly a day goes by when I don't put my feet squarely on the ground and center myself in the ways you taught us, it has been a great help to me. This is important work."

~ Marcus Lang, Priest

"Somatic Consensus practices assist me in following my dreams and contributing to my community and beyond while staying in alignment with my values."

~Hanakyle Morantz, Yoga Teacher and Therapist

"Refreshing and inspiring challenges and ways to search through my internal difficulties and some inspiration to shift out of some of my destructive habits."

~ Forrest Postler

"David provided practices and support for embodied, emotionally aware living."

~ Cameron Withey, Rites of Passage Journeys

"The body and breathing practices I learned re-connected me with my body and literally changed the way I am in the world. I stand straighter and walk with purpose."

~Paul Bartick, Bartick Consulting Group

"I've learned how to listen. How to look someone in the eye, really hear what he or she is saying and experience an empathic connection with him or her."

~Sarah Stafford, College Senior

"I liked the idea that things can be less confusing and less dangerous when you move towards the source of a fight, instead of away."

~ Dylan, age 9

"I liked learning that when you're with someone and caring that if they are attacking, you can pretty much know what they are going to do, before they do it."

~ Devin, age 12

"I liked learning how to walk in a way that I can relate to every thing around me."

~ Annie, age 8

"I felt like a human, not an inmate. I finally was able to sleep. I was able to connect mind and body and that helped me relax."

~ Prison Inmate

What other NVC trainers say

"I was breath-taken and filled with hope connecting to the possibilities of teaching NVC through these examples. It seems that more and more NVC practitioners are including the body in their work; David has his own unique way of doing that and I just hope that as many people as possible could access his work."

~François Beausoleil, CNVC Certified Trainer

"What I experienced very powerfully was (David's) presence and embodiment of NVC consciousness... I enjoyed having movement and experiential learning being center-stage."

~ Lucy Leu, NVC Trainer and author of The NVC Workbook

"I love the opportunity to pay attention to what is happening sensation-wise in the body, to explore what stimulates that, what it means, and how I can become more empowered to choose to better meet my needs based on that awareness. I am still meditating on some of the awarenesses I got from your trainings."

~ Barbara Larson, Certified NVC trainer

"Foremost in my mind is my excitement and joy in how deeply the Aikido movements actually support and facilitate the embodiment of NVC consciousness as I understand and hold it."

~ Loren Swift, Certified NVC Trainer

"David's competence and explanations about psychological and emotional reactions show his level of understanding and respect for the human body. I have longed to see NVC combined with the body! When I shared one move of David's in my NVC classes, one student cried and experienced a shift in consciousness that I saw deepened his NVC understanding and skills throughout the rest of our classes."

~ Taylor Duvall, Therapist, Yoga and NVC instructor

"David's work is versatile, playful and engaging for kids of all ages. He offers tools and a skill set that is valuable for the peaceful navigation and engagement of life, in the classroom, on the playground and at home. We love David. You will love him too."

~ Maren Metke, Teacher—Living Compass School and NVC trainer

Preface

One evening David and I were at a gathering wherein a wise Hawaiian elder was asked to give a blessing. She spoke in a slow, melodious tone—almost a whisper at times—sharing the work she does with troubled youth. She spoke about the damage done to their souls simply because they do not do well in school, and with that one experience they felt stupid, useless and hopeless. In her unhurried tone, she went on to say that we each have a gift to bring to this world, and to find our gift, she said "…you must think.......with your gut". She repeated this two or three times, looking slowly around the room, catching each person's eyes, her voice getting softer and slower each time, "…think (pointing her curved, brown finger to her head), with your gut (bringing her hand down to cover her lower belly).

I found myself in tears as I listened. It was such a simple proclamation, yet filled with the import of the loss we have incurred by how far adrift we have gone from the general neglect of this practice. I realized she was—in one sentence— describing a remedy for healing not only the young ones she was speaking of, but for all of human kind. It was an invocation to trust our gifts, our hearts, our intuitions and the wisdom of our bodies.

So, how do we learn to "think with your gut"?

Becoming What You Need is a map to find our way back to our birthright: our in- heritance of unique gifts and multiple intelligences, to fulfill our potential in the collective brilliance of our humanity. The integration of Aikido, Somatics and Nonviolent Communication offers us cross-training to explore the inconsisten- cies that occur between our hearts and our lips, or what we say and what we do.

These practices can--and often do--touch the grief that we feel when our actions don't match up with who we wish to be, and they also illuminate the incremental shifts to celebrate as we bring our whole selves into alignment, anchored in the language of our hearts.

It requires courage and abundant self-empathy and self-honesty to navigate this path. In these pages we are invited to re-frame our thinking about triggers, to welcome them as an invitation for self-investigation, to locate where a feeling lives in us, what beautiful needs they illuminate, the stories that are enmeshed in the cells and muscles of those feelings, and the beliefs that are born out of those stories. It requires us to be patient and kind with ourselves, and in so doing, learn how to self-regulate so that we can be gentle on ourselves in our becoming what we need.

For we have gotten ourselves into a catastrophic mess from our disconnected thinking. And we can't think our way out of it. I believe that it is in these cross-training practices that we can begin the journey toward healing by fully experiencing the weight of our grief in the strategies that we have employed: from the almost but-not-quite imperceptible hint of dismissal in our tone to a loved one, to the many more obvious acts of collusion in a day that hurtle our earth and all the life it carries toward our possible demise. It is in the full embrace of our precious selves—tragic strategies and all—that we recognize and become response-able to the preciousness of all life and thus, tend to it well.

Try these practices. They may poke, prod, cajole or caress. Whatever form they present themselves in, they invite us to listen to and honor our grief and our praise, our mourning and celebration. In so doing we are brought fully into living gratitude for this breath. This moment. This life. And all that connects us to such abundance.

Judith Weinstock

September, 2017

Table of Contents

The Practices

Inspirations

What we carry emotionally and physically is never far from the foreground of all that we do, perceive, and express, both verbally and nonverbally. To affect real change, we must do more than talk a good game. It requires us to come back, time and time again, to rediscover what we love about the paths we are choosing. Through deliberate, committed, intentional practice over time, we come face to face with the history we've embodied, our deeper self, our greatest gifts, and the motivation to stay the course of becoming the person we choose to be. Somatic Consensus practices for embodying Nonviolent Communication are reconnecting, surprisingly direct, sometimes startling, and always informative.

Two main themes that are woven throughout the all of the practices in this book are:

1. Reclaiming our empathic faculties to recognize and honor the common ground we share in all our relationships, human and nonhuman.

2. Finding and empowering our voices by aligning what we deeply value with our words and actions.

These are essential skills for any of us who want to deepen the quality of our relationships, generate community, and effect positive change—personal, social, environmental, or political. My original work, Somatic Consensus, offers a unique perspective on the NVC basics by focusing on the less-emphasized nonverbal realm in which much communication occurs. The cornerstones that inform the practices of Somatic Consensus are Nonviolent Communication (NVC), Somatic Coaching, the peaceful martial art of Aikido, and lessons gleaned from living the consensus process in my intentional community since 1990. Each brings a unique emphasis, and together, they form the practices in this book for synchronizing language, emotions, and actions to support a meaningful life that is deeply felt.

We are always feeling something. How we discern and act upon what we feel connects or disconnects us from opportunities that are available to enrich our lives. From intimate relationships to international politics, the consequences of not paying enough attention to what we feel are evident, and the cause originates from the deep mistrust of our own bodies. We see daily messages that commercialize and distance us from our bodies, instead of acknowledging the body as a source of learning and an ever-present wealth of information about ourselves.

This schism leads to a long procession of incoherent and destructive personal and communal patterns. For many years, participants in my trainings, my friends, and especially my wife Judith have urged me to write a book to share this somatic approach for embodying NVC. Based on the work of Marshall Rosenberg, NVC's core teachings illuminate how our feelings put us in touch with our deeper, universal human needs, and that when these become the source of our words and actions, we create conditions conducive to enriching relation-ships through compassionate exchange.

Cornerstones

Much of my adult life has been dedicated to fostering relationships and com-munities where all voices are valued and in which everyone thrives. This com- mitment took on a world of new challenges in 1990 when Judith and I joined eight other families to start the intentional community in which we live and raised our family. Our common vision—to steward the land, share resources wherever possible, and care for our children more collaboratively— made all the sense in the world back then and still holds true for us today. Determined and filled with a sense of purpose, the other co-founders, along with Judith and , walked into the tasks of community with the best intentions. The struggles and trials during our community's formative years were plentiful and took us far beyond our comfort zones. In those early days, our community felt like a pressure cooker of relationships in a house of mirrors, with relentless reflections of our-selves in one another's eyes.

At one particular time when we were desperate to find better ways to work through our differences, one of my neighbors organized a weekend NVC workshop. This introductory workshop brought up more questions than it answered, but the power in its principles was evident, so we pursued it further.

Soon after, at another workshop, I was given the instruction to sit and listen with empathy to two women who were engaged in a role-playing conflict. At the time, I found the explanations of empathy somewhat vague, so I filled things in with my imagination. As the role-playing got underway, the women began to argue. I quieted my breath and thoughts and imagined a listening field as a bubble around me that grew to include, feel, and gently hold the two women with care. This produced a heightened sensitivity that allowed me to sense heartfelt needs beneath the two women's heated words. The space around us felt charged with an aliveness that bridged the distance between us. Something felt familiar, and then I was struck with an epiphany. This is Aikido! I realized that empathy in NVC was the same as a "ki field" in Aikido, and that giving empathy to these two women was something I had been practicing for 20 years while training in that peaceful martial art. From that moment on, I began finding ways these two traditions for harmonizing conflict could inform each other. NVC offers an elegant language to those who study Aikido, and Aikido lends kinesthetic elements to every aspect of NVC.

Similar to NVC, encoded within all Aikido practices is the intention of loving protection for all. Aikido training develops the ability to be skillfully empathic in the face of intensifying conflict. Not unlike the "force" in the famous Star Wars movies, one of the more esoteric core aspects of Aikido is training with ki. When someone attacks in Aikido training, the experienced student learns to center and expand his or her attention to surround the attacker with an intention of loving protection, an energetic ki field, much like I did with the two women in the NVC role-playing exercise. When you include another in such a way, it becomes possible to sense the intentions and needs at the core of another's aggressive words or actions, and by doing so, to harmonize the "attack" at its source, before it has time to turn to violence.

Aikido's time-honored tradition of mastery strengthens and harmonizes mind, body, and spirit. It introduces exciting, kinesthetic ways to practice and embody NVC principles. These complimentary linguistic and kinesthetic paths merge perfectly within the field of Somatics. Somatics address how repetitive responses to life's situations become lodged in our nervous systems and muscles, along with the promise of intentional recurrent practice in learning new skills. Somatics illuminate how tuning directly into our sensory experience informs our cognitive understanding so that we can:

- *Participate deeply in our own healing,*
- *Discharge the anxiety held in old embodied reactions,*
- *Contact deep needs that have been habitually ignored, and*
- *Cultivate resources for connecting with one another more capably and enjoyably.*

Somatics is the art and practice of sensing mind and body as experienced from within. When we train our attention to shift from the dramas that we perceive to the instinctual wisdom of our bodies, our bodies become a place to come home to whenever we lose our bearings.

Our bodies put us in touch with our emotions, and our emotions—when consciously listened to—tell us what matters and what we need. Embodying NVC in daily practice focuses attention on the signals of our bodies and the present, direct, immediate experience of the life we are living. This is where we can access discriminating wisdom, develop reverence for the sacred, and where we feel the suffering and grief that give birth to compassion. Here is where we can regain our footing again and again as we walk into the mystery of life and love.

How to Use This Book

This book provides a basic blueprint of practical tools for cultivating healthy personal and group relationships. These tools support life-enriching choices that are rooted in sensing one's needs and balancing them with the needs of others, speaking your truth and being receptive to others within the bonds of relationship. These are important and learnable skills.

Whether you are a first-day beginner or an advanced trainer, I hope you will find this kinesthetic approach valuable. The stories and practices are designed to spark your imagination and invite your participation, because what you practice must capture your imagination to sustain your interest over the long haul. Practice is where the rubber meets the road and change occurs. So play, muster your curiosity, try creative variations on these themes, and work with the forms of the practices to make them your own.

Somatic practices touch on places below our cognitive radar, so even if the practices do not make sense, I encourage you to try them and see where they take you. The more slowly and mindfully you practice the exercises, the better. As you deepen your practice, you will notice ways that all of the practices in this book intersect and support one another. This approach, from passive to active participant, is a necessity for embodying what you learn on the path of becoming what you need.

Knowing others is
intelligence; knowing yourself
is true wisdom. Mastering
others is strength, mastering
yourself is true power.

Lao Tzu

CHAPTER ONE

Understanding Power

Understanding power begins with a question to oneself, "What do I really care about? Knowing the ground that you stand on as you listen and get to know where another stands is where "understanding" that empowers all is found. In school, were you ever asked, "What do you care about?" or how about, "What would you love to learn today?" Most of us were never asked questions like these growing up. I wasn't, and only a fraction of the participants in my workshops remember such queries. Instead, most of us grew up with the "practice" of choosing what to study from a narrow group of subjects and learning to depend on grades for approval from others to feed our self-worth, sense of belonging, and sense of security. By practice, I refer to how we learn to embody new habits and skills through the repetition of specific thoughts, feelings, and actions over time. Over time, the practice of living for the approval of others can become a form of self-tyranny. Looking outside ourselves without feeling a connection to what we care about and where true power originates, may well be the single most significant reason for the high rate of breakdowns in personal relationships, depression, the lack of job satisfaction, and violence. We are in our power whenever we live the qualities that give meaning to our mutual lives. The ennobling qualities we choose and intentionally practice such as integrity, honesty, empathy, and compassion create better alignment, less constriction, and more tolerance for enhanced energy in order to better process power.

When Judith and I first began to learn Nonviolent Communication, we invited practice groups to our home for weekly sessions. Afterward, as we debriefed, invariably we'd start to argue. As our habitual power dynamics emerged we watched all the wonderful skills we thought we had learned fly out the window. We'd co-lead a two-hour class, and then afterwards invariably quarrel for two more. We discovered how nearly impossible it can be to listen empathetically if we're both triggered and in emotional pain. After many years of marriage and leading workshops together, it can still get awkward and comical navigating some of our arguments when we fall into "using" NVC language on one another *without* the consciousness. Always a work in progress, the consciousness underlying NVC is resourced through empathic connection to our mutual needs. Marshall Rosenberg speaks of "needs" as the energy of life—something divine— that we all share. I use the term "common ground" as a metaphor for understanding mutual needs. Paying close attention to the mutual needs underlying our own and others' feelings and actions in order to create compassionate connection is key to the practice of NVC.

In significant relationships, as well as on any path of mastery and self-mastery, conflicts will arise in the process of change in the form of our resistance to change. Any resistance that attempts to ignore conflict will obscure what the conflict is there to illuminate. There is a power that is undeniably felt and that leaves little to resist when words and actions arise from our common ground.

There is harmony to be found in the center of every conflict, but to find it re-quires centering oneself and strategies that are connective, not forceful.

Like draws like and force creates counter-force. When what you do comes from what you care about, actions become more organized, less forceful and more powerfully moving. Somatically, power and force have different origins and very different outcomes. When we are connected to and move from our deepest needs and what we truly care about, and put that out into the world, we are in our true power.

Power vs. Force Exploration

Here is an exploration that offers a visceral sense of our true power and the potency of moving from a compassionate consciousness. Before you start, read through all of the directions. Be sensitive and proceed carefully and slowly with your partner. Inform one another about any injuries, sensitivities, or weak spots that may get in the way of the practice.

Person A: Stand on the side and slightly to the front of Person B. Ask your partner to put his or her wrist on your shoulder. *Make sure your partner's elbow is facing down so it does not get injured.*

Person B: Make a fist, straighten and stiffen your arm. Say out loud, "I will not let you bend my arm." This represents a fighting stance—offensive or defensive.

Person A: Put both hands on the upper crease of your partner's elbow and firmly, without jerking and very slowly, attempt to bend the arm. Remember, this is a muscle test, not a competition. It is not about seeing who is stronger or if you can bend your partner's arm, because sometimes you can't. This is about noticing and comparing the amount of force each of you must employ in your part of this exercise.

Part Two:

Person A: Stand on the side and slightly to the front of your partner. Take person B's arm and lift it up to rest on your shoulder—*again, with her elbow pointed down to avoid injury*. This time, make sure that your partner's arm is relaxed and that she is not helping you lift her arm. You will find that some people cannot not help. If you feel her muscles tense up at

all, coach her by saying, " Give me your arm," and with a gentle shake, " I have you." Let her know that tightening her muscles will restrict the flow of her power.

Person B: Think about something or someone you truly love. Breathe into your belly. Imagine the love in your belly as a glowing coal. And breathing gently fan the flame of that love so that it gradually fills your torso. Don't rush the process.

As it continues to grow, let it fill up your arm as if it were a fire hose. Fire hoses become incredibly stiff as water courses through them. Tensing your muscles will contract the hose and block the flow, so keep your arm as relaxed and open as possible.

While keeping your arm relaxed, open, and without tension, imagine the energy of your loving intention, like a fire hydrant pouring out from your core, flowing through your body, arm and fingers. Let your hand and fingers fill up like a balloon and then release the pressure by shooting it out toward and then past the horizon. Let the energy flow with purpose. Let your partner know when you are ready.

Person B: Put both of your hands on the upper crease of your partner's elbow and firmly, without jerking, attempt to bend her arm. Debrief and then switch roles.

As you debrief, notice the differences between parts 1 and 2 in the actual strength of the arm you are trying to bend. How do both persons A and B experience this? What do you notice in the difference between muscling and fullness, force and power?

Power is that which supports the significance of life itself. It arises from the kind of meaning revealed through being courageously honest with one self. Force creates counterforce and is limited by that. Force is movement against opposition. Force most often shows up where real power is absent. It's very curious and surprising to experience how when we are relaxed, open, and inclusive, we are even more powerful than when we are rigid, tight, and contracted. How would this feel in relationship? When you resist or fight another—represented in this practice when you say " I will not let you bend my arm"—you are using a good portion of your resources on offense or defense. If defense and offense are two opposite sides of a continuum, what is directly between them?   Connection.

THE S.U.R.F. CENTERING PRACTICE

In the practices for embodying NVC, each word that expresses a need becomes a somatic exploration, a welcome signpost pointing toward something much more expansive. The S.U.R.F. Centering practice is a simple and expansive meditative practice for exploring the qualities of needs in great depth. Over time, it increases the ability to articulate and integrate thoughts with feelings, clear emotional blockage, and, embody and extend an empathic listening field imbued with ennobling qualities. The acronym S.U.R.F. stands for Shape, Unify, Resource, and Field. Read the whole S.U.R.F. Practice and the descriptions accompanying each step, then sink into the simplicity of the essential practice synopsized at the end. It can be slowly and quietly explored as a sitting practice. Once you've learned its steps, it also can be done anywhere, at any time, in just a few seconds. Keep it simple. To begin with, pick just one quality. You can take a look at the needs list in Appendix B for some qualities to explore.

Step One: Shape

How you shape yourself affects how you feel, how you listen, what you perceive, how you learn, what you communicate, and how you're received. First sit in your full vertical length with your head above heart above belly. Let your skeleton hold you in this alignment with gravity as it is meant to do. If you lean, slouch, or overextend, you are fighting gravity and using more muscle than you need to.

- Relax and settle into your full length.

- Let your jaw go, and let the back of your tongue relax on the floor of your mouth.

- Let your shoulders drop, as if any weight you may be carrying in your life just rolls off. Just put it to the side for now. (Not to worry. When the practice is over, you can put it back on your shoulders if you like.)

- Let your sphincter (butt) muscles relax. Feel your sit bone connect to your seat and to the earth.

Step Two: Unify

Take one or two long, slow, settling and unifying breaths. As you breathe out, open your mouth and make an audible "*Ahhhh.*"

For the rest of this practice, visualize a circular breathing pattern where the "in" breath goes up your back and the "out" breath goes down your front. Let your belly be relaxed.

Step Three: Re-source

Take a moment to consider and choose a word that represents one quality you would love to have a little more of in your life, such as acceptance, respect, joy, courage, understanding, appreciation, belonging, gratitude, empathy or any other quality you're interested in exploring (See needs list in Appendix B). In time, you can mix and explore combinations of these qualities, but for now, choose one.

- Ask your body—soma, "What would it be like if I felt a little more__?" Fill in the blank with a quality/need. Give yourself time and space to allow your body/soma to respond. In the time between asking a question and get- ting an answer, there is a moment of not knowing, a state of openness. Stay with it. Breathe and drop your attention into your body. Let your body shape itself and inform you. Try not to have a mental idea of the responses before they come. Live with the question while the heart dances with the answer.

- Notice any subtle changes in posture, breath, body temperature, mood, muscles, etc. Notice any stories, thoughts, or feelings that arise.

Sometimes it is difficult to understand, trust, or even imagine the qualities you wish to learn because either you are unfamiliar with them or there is some internal resistance that gets in the way. There may be times when you choose a quality such as "gratitude" or "joy" but don't know what it is like to feel gratitude or   are in such pain that joy is hard to imagine. If this occurs, you might think of a person you know or a character you've seen in a movie or read about who has such a quality and then try it on for yourself.

You may encounter times when calling up a quality may startle you by stirring up some historical emotional response. For example, you may find yourself feeling tight when you try to imagine a little more " acceptance" because of some moral judgments you tell yourself, such as " I am not worthy of love" or " I should be smarter." S.U.R.F. can be a daily practice of self-empathy that eventually turns old reactions into resources for healing and connection. Proceed gently and slow- ly, paying close attention to your body's sense of what is too much and what is too little. If you find yourself contracting or uncomfortable in any way, muster the courage of heart to remain open and curious about why this may be so. If you hit a strong contractive emotional response, you can shift the question to:

"How would it feel if I felt just a tiny bit more_____?"

If this is still too triggering, ask yourself for only a fraction of the quality that you previously requested. If that is too much, then try half of that and so on until you come to a threshold that is acceptable where you can feel a shift. The quiet and safe moments that you sit in the S.U.R.F. Practice are a good time and place to get to know the emotional pain that contracts your body when historical self-talk and fears arise. So take care to be gentle with self-judgments. Give them just the light of your attention, then let them go.

Step Four: Field

Breathe into the feelings, slowly and gently, as you fill up your torso and appendages with the quality you are imagining in Step 3. Bring your attention to the space a few feet all around you—in front of you, behind, above, below, and then to the sides of you. You can imagine you are in the center of a bubble. Equalize your attention all around you. Imagine the quality and the way it feels filling your body and then filling the space in the bubble around you. This is an empathic field of attention. From your sitting practice, continue to hold the field as you get up to start your day. The point is not to be in this centered place all the time; it is to come back to it often. From time to time during the day you can expand your bubble to listen to others with the qualities you choose.

Notice how the space around you is enlivened just by how you focus your attention.

In the course of the day, slowly and mindfully, practice holding others in your field. Some people you might listen to in a field of gratitude, others compassion, others joy, others creativity, and so on. *If it is too overwhelming to call up a specific need or to hold others in your field, appreciate this as good information and an appropriate time to move more slowly, patiently, and compassionately on your journey to understand the source of your core habits and strategies. (See Core Contractive Strategies page 72).

If you are training with others, try this: Turn to the person nearest to you and imagine expanding your bubble in all directions. As it contacts the other person, imagine it expanding a little farther to include your partner. Keep the bubble open, and as you hold each other in it, share something about yourself that the other does not know. Keep it simple, and notice the quality of empathic connection you feel.

The Essential Practice

1. **Shape** - Let your skeleton hold you up in alignment with gravity - head above heart and heart above belly.

2. **Unify** - Take a long slow breath in and then on the exhale, release a relaxing "Ahhh." Do it again.

3. **Resource** - As you ask your body the following question, allow a moment for an answer to arise: What would it be like if I felt a bit more? (Fill in a quality—just one). Notice the shifts in your body? Just notice.

4. **Field** - Imagine the feeling of the quality filling up the space within and then two to three feet around you.

SHAPE-SHIFTING PRACTI(

William Blake said, "But to the eyes of the man of imagin₂
nation itself. As a man is so he sees." Carl Jung defined nei
nature. Somatics mends that divide with a new story: we are
and a body—we are an inter-reliant, intelligent, and social b
experiences, environment, history, interaction, and genetics.   , , we see messages that commercialize and distance us from our bodies instead of
acknowledging the body as a source of learning and an ever-present wealth of
information about ourselves.

This is a practice that involves five elements that, when engaged through our
imagination and explored over time, develops " somatic impressions"—whole
body/mind understandings that reveal the expansive nature of the qualities of
needs such as:

Understanding and meaning	*Ground*
Belonging and empathy	*Water*
Lightness and joy	*Wind*
Creativity and expression	*Fire*
Presence and clarity	*Space*

Each element provides an opportunity for profound insights and self-growth.
This practice adds visualization and linguistic features inspired by Dr. Stuart
Heller's creative Tai Chi teachings. It is designed to increase resourcefulness,
clarity, and versatility. Versatility is the ability to bring forth a way of being,
thinking, feeling, and responding that best fits the situation and the people you
are with. As you practice, pay close attention to sensations, feelings, the
shapes, and any internal shifts in your body.

First get to know the shapes and intentions in the sequence described below.
Over time, change the sequence, and adapt the shapes and qualities to your own
liking. As you become more familiar with each element, your body will, like
a divining rod, inform you and flow more easily toward the essential wisdom
found in each element. Practice on both your right side and left side. Practice as
quickly or as slowly as you want, spending a few seconds to a few minutes in
each position. As though you are an actor moving into different roles, explore the
feelings and sensations, how your breath changes, and the stories that come up
for you in each position. Discover the relationships among these elements as you
flow and shift between them. Remember to practice all these elemental shapes on
both your right and left sides.

Let's Begin

...me an open, vertical stance, with head above heart and ...eart above belly. Take a relaxing breath as you settle into your full length, not too stiff and not collapsed.

The body and its wondrous ecosystem offer us a direct connection to the life around and within us, but we must first know where we stand. Knowing the ground that you stand on as you listen and get to know the ground where another stands is where "under-standing" is found.

Ground
Meaning, Clarity, Understanding

With your left foot forward, bend your legs slightly to move a little closer to the earth. Place your hands by your sides and about a foot in front of you. Open your palms so they face the ground, and spread your fingers apart. Keep your body vertical, head above heart above belly. Move your whole body Connect your circuitry with the circuitry of the earth and in your own way, muster a sense of gratitude for the ground that is supporting you—under each of us—and that brings understanding.

Here are some grounding questions to consider as you shape to ground yourself:

> What do I deeply care about?
> What is the ground I stand on?
> What brings meaning to my life?
> What can't I truly get enough of?

Each day, move to the ground position and articulate what you care about in a word or sentence. Begin with the qualities you stand on such as honesty, integrity, equality, playfulness, respect, etc. Feel for the word(s) that most represent what you most value. The clearer your choice(s), the more it becomes an organizing principle for your life.

Next, begin to shape a short sentence, such as, "I care about dignity" or "I care about honesty, integrity and compassion."

Ground your statement with "for the sake of" phrases. For example, "I care about honesty, integrity and compassion for the sake of contributing to a better world for my children to flourish in."

Declare the ground that you stand on—and why that matters—in words that resonate and inspire you. Whether it is one word or a sentence that expresses a quality, a need, or a commitment, let your expression grow and evolve to invigorate your whole being.

Water
Fluidity, Belonging, Adaptability

As you move from ground to water, shift your body back and down. Bring your left foot (which is currently forward in the ground position) back so it is now behind your right foot.

Behind: Open your hands and bring them slightly behind you, to your sides and with palms facing back. Place your attention behind you and appreciate the resources to be found there: the teachers in your life, past and present, great teachers of our world, ancestors who were healthy and whole, and our genetic history.

At first, when learning this practice, choose one person and the quality they embody to explore over time. Imagine him or her at your back, and since you are mostly space, you might visualize the quality you admire coming through you. Chapter 13, the Ecology of Relationship, explores the practice of honoring ancestors and drawing forth the vast resources at our backs. Finding those at your back is not about having someone who is without flaw to draw from. There is no one who fits that bill. The practice here is to identify one quality in each person you admire and not to weigh and balance this quality against other qualities they also may have or lack. If you cannot find anyone to represent the quality you wish to cultivate, use your imagination to make someone up. One possibility is to imagine someone you saw in a movie or read about in a book.

To your sides: Slowly move your arms out to the sides as you gather and appreciate those who walk beside you in this life. Your friends, brothers, sisters, partners, and associates make up a social width that extends far to your left and right. As with those at your back, be discerning so as not to overwhelm your system. For starters, invite one at a time. With practice, you can invite and get to know your more challenging relationships, the ones that have the potential to shed light on places in you that others do not.

The young ones who walk in front of you: Turn your palms forward, and in a gathering motion, bring your arms and hands forward. Imagine gathering what is behind and at your sides to connect with what is in front of you. Appreciate those younger ones whom you support and who keep us connected to innocence, beauty, and the importance of play. Perhaps the teenager reminds you of your fierce desire for autonomy. You may recall the playfulness of a child when you find yourself in a situation that feels dense, heavy, or boring. As we connect with the younger ones we connect to a wider horizon of meaning that extends into the future beyond our own lifetime.

In time and with practice you can begin to empathize with more challenging individuals around you, past and present. Seek out their humanity and learn to appreciate their qualities and your common ground. The internal connective dialogues are limitless. Water brings rest and solace in knowing you are always connected with all your relationships.

Remember, the more you employ your imagination and can find your gratitude for those all around you, both past and present—all your relations—the more resources become available.

As you transition from water to fire bring your arms wide out in front of your chest. This movement gathers all that is behind, to the side and in front of you and comes to an open stance. Reach out with open hands and fingers as if you're about to catch a beach ball. This is an open stance that both receives and offers. When you speak from this shape, it comes out of a place of fullness.

When you know the common ground you stand on and are grateful for all your relations, it becomes easier to move with power and the fire of compassion.

Fire
Expression, Creativity, Decisiveness

Now bring your left foot in front again, the same stance you held in the ground position. Bring your hands to eye level, hands flat, and palms toward each other about a foot in front of you. Now bring your right hand forward enough so that your left thumb is a few inches from your right hand's pinky finger. Imagine that your hands are like a sword and you are preparing to cut or clear your way with this sword. Open your hands and point your fingers toward the sky with the blades of your hands reaching, pushing forward. Extend your arms, with just a slight bend at the elbow.

As you move the blades of your hands in front of you, bring them to a place that is not too close to your body and not over extended away from your torso. If the blades of your hands are too close to your body, connection to others becomes weak. If your blades are too far from your torso, you become disconnected from your core. In this practice of fire, your blades are there to cut away what is unnecessary, to make room for what serves life. Just as a sculptor uses sharp tools to create beauty, sometimes you must cut away things in your life to manifest the beauty you want. You can ask yourself, "What do I need to cut away for the sake of what I deeply value?" Then make your cut with honesty and clarity. Knowing where you stand as you connect with the resources that are around you can help to relax your system. The more relaxed you are, the more aware you can be and the better you can express your own truth with dignity and graciousness. (For a more comprehensive look at the Fire Practice see the Choosing Decisively practice on page 57).

Wind
Autonomy, Joy, Playfulness, Ease

Don't take what others say personally. Let some of it go by.
Lighten up.

It's easy to get overloaded by trying to take on too much. Wind helps to feel and discern what is too much for our systems to handle, regulate what we take in, and what we need to let go of. This practice helps us to differentiate clearly between what others say and what we hear. Practices teaches how to not take what others say and do quite so personally. This is explored in more depth within the Spiral Blend Practice on page 145). From the fire stance, turn your body sideways. Like a matador evading a charging bull, turn to the side and step slightly back and off the line of attack. With your feet now directly below each shoulder and pointing forward, spread your arms and hands wide as if you were a bird soaring. In the wind position, let whatever is coming at you—a thought, a word, a fist—go by. Move your head

to first see where it is coming from, turn your head to follow it as if it were a train passing by, and then turn your head again to see where it came from and then follow where it is going. Bring a lightness and buoyancy to this shape and movement; let it evoke a sense of joy and freedom.

Wind is a freeing element and one we often forget to access. As you get more adept at moving between elements, remember that if you feel stuck and don't know what to do, go to wind and imagine whatever is overwhelming you blowing by. Let it go by, and remember not to take another person's pain on as your own.

Space
Presence, Empathy, Equanimity

Come back to the opening stance, with both feet directly under your shoulders. With head above heart above belly, breathe deeply while you imagine and explore the quality of spaciousness within and around you. Feel your presence. This is the shape of being open to this present moment. Breathing and settle into the shape of this element gets us out of our own way to allow empathy, curiosity, and intuition to arise.

All the other elements center us to be more present. Space happens between all the other elements. Space is the connective tissue for all that is going on. Including another in your spaciousness is the essence of empathy. The element of space is critical for empathic communication and is explored throughout many of the following chapters.

The Light and Shadow

We all move between each of these five elements—ground, water, fire, wind, and space. At the same time, we tend to practice certain ones more than others. Each element has advantages and drawbacks, light and shadow sides for any given moment.

Which is your predominant element, and which do you practice least?

Ground—Do you see yourself as a person who's really solid, firm in what you care about, and grounded in what you love and know? You can align yourself with the earth to find centered, beauty, and balance as you walk on your path. Some qualities associated with ground are meaning, stability, understanding, and focus.

Shadow side of ground—Stubbornness

Water—Are you adaptive, calming, fluid, and do you have a strong sense of belonging and connection within yourself and in relationships? Water is the ocean of relationships, the medium of empathy, love, and greater acceptance. Some qualities associated with water are belonging, flowing, inclusivity, empathy, acceptance, and harmony.

Shadow side of water—Indecisiveness

Fire—Are you expressive, creative, and focused? Fire moves with purpose and power. Fire purifies. It is stimulating and expansive. Fire speaks with honesty and clarity. Some qualities of fire are action with decisiveness, powerful expression, creativity, and focused attention.

Shadow side—Explosive, overly intense

Wind—Are you playful? Do you have a lightness of being that does not get hung-up or too attached to what other people are saying or doing? In wind we gain a higher perspective. By moving from "me" centered to a sense of "we" consciousness, wind can be freeing and uplifting. Some qualities of wind are lightness, vision, ease, joy, and freedom.

Shadow side—Brittle, ungrounded, air-headed

Space—Are you often present to the moment? Do you breathe deeply and feel relaxed and accepting? Space allows room to move, to contemplate, and to not feel rushed or constricted. Some qualities of space are openness, centered, being relaxed, spacious, and present.

Shadow side—Spacey, not present

As you go about your day, notice how your thoughts and feelings are affected by the wind or cold on a winter day. Do they become more clear or crisp? How does it feel to walk with a little more gratitude for the ground you stand on? Notice which element seems most meaningful to you, which ones feel most familiar, which ones you relate to most, and which ones you relate to least. Enjoy exploring the deeper nuances of each element.

Each element can teach you about your larger purpose in life by affirming your harmony with nature. Discover for yourself how these elements relate to one another—each is a facet of the same gem. You are made of the same elements as the earth—carbon, oxygen, nitrogen, and hydrogen. Your body is a microcosm of the patterns of the earth, and the first unit of localism, upon which your home, town, and greater community are built. Graciously inhabiting your body fully honors all definitions of community.

Only one who devotes himself to a cause with his whole strength and soul can be a true master. For this reason mastery demands all of a person.

Albert Einstein

CHAPTER TWO

Somatic Practice

At times, we live in ways that cultivate only a part of who we are. When this is the case, the life in us is squeezed into a shape that is not fully our own.

In spite of this, deeper currents assert the needs in us that are calling to be nourished. In any given moment, we connect with or disconnect from these currents depending on the choices we make and what we practice. We are always practicing something, whether we are conscious of it or not. This is how we learn or, alternatively, how we reinforce old habits.

Intentional somatic practice is an agent of change that can assist us in embedding consciously chosen habits into our being and in replacing old habits and patterns we have previously developed that may no longer serve us. Any true path we choose requires us to rediscover, time and time again, what we love about the path we are choosing; and, through deliberate, committed, and intentional practice, to embody the skills we need and the qualities we choose to live.

Two things that affect the depth of learning and connection we experience in our practice are the intention we bring to it and the degree to which we inhabit the forms of what we practice. For example, there is form to the physical act of shaking hands. We set the shape and imbue the form with our intention. Our unique histories; what we have practiced; our fears, hopes, stories, desires, cultures, and so forth, make each handshake unique. Shake a limp hand, and there is no life transmitted through the structure. Shake a hand that is stiff and muscled, and it becomes difficult to make a heartfelt connection. If the handshake is imbued with the intention for connection and a welcoming desire for inclusiveness, the shape and structure of the handshake breathes life into the form and becomes a conduit for generative relationships. It is the same with NVC. The language constructs, techniques, forms, and practices can be either aids or detriments to connection, depending on the consciousness and intention with which they are imbued. In other words, we embody whatever intention we imbue our practices with.

As with any art, the basic forms of NVC (Appendix A), once embodied, must be let go of, or communication can become mechanical, disconnecting and rote. We can always apply the formulas when grasping to connect with one another in conflict, but the task is to embody the practices in order to make them authentically, creatively our own. The emergent field of Somatics sheds some light on the basics of mastery and the art of embodying a practice.

The Basics

1. Identify what you care about (Needs).
2. Notice what you have practiced in your life (Strategies).
3. Choose practices that align with your deep needs.
4. Practice who you want to become in the world.

1. Identify What You Care About. Marshall Rosenberg said that practice can become sterile without clear purpose (intention). The first lesson on traversing any path toward mastery is to make practices meaningful. Aligning what we practice with what we care about invests our practice with meaning. The next step is to make practice enjoyable and interesting. Any artful training, if not attuned to the deeper intentions of the practice, lacks power and progresses only so far. The more we love what we are doing, the more relevant our practices become and the longer they endure.

2. Notice What You Have Practiced in Your Life. What do you do repeatedly? How do you respond to conflict? What do you resist, and what draws you? As you notice your conscious and unconscious habits, discern which ones support what you care about and which ones do not.

What we resist will persist. In the process of trying to shift away from old, uncon- scious strategies that no longer support us, it is helpful to consciously identify and accept our resistance. Doing this lays bare the challenges that the changes our practices are moving us through create. In other words, resistance can be viewed as a signpost that points us toward our histories and the information we need in order to do things better.

3. Choose practices that align with your deep needs. Once we can articulate what really matters and want to move toward, we can shape and commit to deliberate, rigorous practices that, over time, develops in us specific skills that will take us where we want to go. Here we ask ourselves, "What are the specific and doable practices I must commit to in order to achieve my goal?" Extending the breadth and depth of the practices we consciously choose—emotionally, intellectually, and spiritually—empowers any true path of mastery. Older wisdom traditions around the world consider their ancestors and future generations in the important choices they make.

4. Practice Who It Is You Want to Become. Remind yourself regularly what and why you are practicing. Peel away distractions and diversions. Check in with the stories and narratives you tell yourself. Strip away ego investment, and leave behind what others think. Practice with intention, and then notice what happens. Most importantly, be playful and imaginative to make it enjoyable. Just as it is possible to build our muscles with weight training or running, we can build the "muscles" of integrity, honesty, graciousness, and dignity on any noble path we choose.

Building New Neural Pathways

Michelangelo, the great Renaissance artist, once said, "If people only knew how hard I work to gain my mastery, it wouldn't seem so wonderful at all." Modern science is finally catching up with the time-honored traditions of mastery. New research shows that outstanding performance is the product of years of deliberate practice, not of any innate talent or skill, and that our brains are living structures with infinite possibilities. Recent studies suggest that muscle memory comes with 300 repetitions, embodiment takes 3,000 repetitions, and mastery takes 10,000 hours of practice. Whether it is the artist's brush stroke, a skilled sushi chef wield- ing a knife, a seasoned martial artist executing a throw, or the embodiment of NVC, mastery comes through intentional and committed practice, practice, practice.

A revolutionary new discovery in neuroscience illuminates how this kind of practice looks and how *myelin* increases the speed and capacity of learning
pathways in our brains. The brain and spinal cord are made up of many cells, including neurons. About 100 billion neurons send and receive electrochemical signals to and from the brain and nervous system. Neurons vary in length from a fraction of an inch to several feet. Myelin is a white sheathing that coats the neural cells in our brains along pathways developed for specific tasks. Intentional and deep practice stimulates myelin to grow and wrap around the neuron fibers that fire along specific neuronal routes. As myelin grows, it

insulates the pathways, and this increases the speed, strength, and accuracy of the signals flowing through the neurons. When Albert Einstein died, scientists studied his brain and found a great deal of this white matter. At the time, they did not know what myelin was, but now we do.

The key practices that produce myelin and build neural pathways are:

> *1. Ignition.*
>
> *2. Get a big picture.*
>
> *3. Break it down, slow it down.*
>
> *4. Make corrections, learn from your mistakes, do it again, repeat regularly.*
>
> *5. Become familiar with your learning edge.*

1. Ignition. Ignition is that initial spark when something grabs us and we say, "I want to do that." Since he was a toddler, my youngest son, Sam, would run around and move his body to any music he heard. When he was nine, we took him to see a performance that was written, directed, and performed by Savion Glover, quite likely the greatest tap dancer who ever lived. The performance ignited Sam. Immediately afterward, we went out and bought him tap shoes, and from that day on, Sam did not walk, he tapped.

*Take a moment to remember a time in your life when you felt a flash of ignition.

2. Get a Big Picture. When Sam first saw Savion perform, something inside him envisioned possibilities of rhythms he could make with his feet, the joy he would find, and the beauty he might share. The power of that big picture gave him a destination with a staying power that has never waned. Ignition and getting a big picture provides the "through line" to get from here to there.

*Can you recall a big picture moment you had of something you wanted to do, create, or become? How did it shape your life?

3. Break It Down, Slow It Down. Sam decided he wanted tap lessons, and all roads led to Cheryl Johnson's tap studio in downtown Seattle. When you experience mastery embodied in someone, you can feel it. Cheryl was a pro. She was part of the renowned tap-dancing duo Johnson and Peters. Her art was cellular; her love of tap was soulful. Sam loved to watch her dance. She inspired him. She would show Sam a routine, then he would slow it down and break it down into learn-able segments, practicing it over and over.

*Watch a toddler's slow pace and processes when learning how to walk or talk. This is how we learn.

4. Make Corrections, Learn from Mistakes, Do It Again, Repeat Reg- ularly. Mistakes—those same experiences that we have been taught to avoid— are essential to growing myelin. Sam would break down each new routine into learnable chunks and then practice, correct, practice, correct, again and again. Whenever he added or missed a tap, he stopped, corrected, and started again.

*Re-frame mistakes as opportunities to learn and appreciate what worked and what didn't.

5. Become Familiar with Your Learning Edge. "Reach" is to strain to- ward that which is just beyond one's current ability. It is a sweet yet bitter place. Most people who reach a level of mastery have learned to appreciate and enjoy feeling that edge. The brain is designed to conserve energy and feels uncomfort- able doing new things. Practicing with just enough stress to manage change is ex- actly the kind of practice that builds myelin. The learning edge is that sweet spot between what we know and what we would love to learn. Purposefully changing old, ingrained ways of being necessitates a certain amount of discomfort. The strangeness of doing something different from what you have historically done can bring up buried pain, struggles, and old memories, so expect any depthful practice to be something of a love/hate relationship. Trying to learn new things too quickly can overload your system, and when that happens, the learning does not sink in. Learn to pace yourself and be willing to leave your comfort zone. New practices, even positive ones, do not feel comfortable until they become habits, usually after 30 days of continuous practice.

*Go slightly beyond your comfort zone to struggle through learning new skills, then repeat until you can do it more and more correctly, over and over.

Beginner's Mind

Marshall Rosenberg often said, "Don't do anything that you do not experience as play." In his inimitable and succinct way, Marshall was sharing his under- standing of what I understand as "beginner's mind."

There is an old Zen story that tells of a professor in Buddhist studies who came to study with a Zen master. After making the customary bows, he asked her to teach him Zen, then began to talk about his extensive doctrinal background. The professor kept trying to hold up whatever the master shared against his own scholarly notions of the way the world is and how it ought be. The master listened patiently, then began to make tea. When it was ready, he poured the tea into the scholar's cup until it began to overflow onto the floor. When the professor noticed what was happening, he shouted: "Stop, stop! The cup is full. You can't fill it anymore." The master replied, "Yes, I know." The master stopped pouring and said: "You are like this cup. You are full of ideas. If you truly seek understanding, then first, empty your cup!"

When we empty ourselves, let go, and cease to hold tightly to our views, the truth will come to us. We Westerners cherish our opinions and find this attitude difficult because we have been brought up to value rational thought processes above all else. This attitude is deeply embedded and forms the basis for much of our way of life. Beginner's mind is an attitude of openness, eagerness, curiosity, and a lack of preconceptions when studying a subject—even when studying at an advanced level—just as a true beginner in that subject would.

Sometimes setting aside the knowledge you have worked hard to gain takes a great deal of courage. Are you willing to be confused in order to find clarity? Are you willing to make mistakes, to face yourself regardless of the truth you see or the emotions it stirs up? A beginner's mind is an attitude of wonder that is open and curious to learn and discover. It's a mindset that deepens any practice.

Chinese philosopher Lao Tzu said, "Wise men hear and see as little children do." Beginner's mind is an attitude of humility and deep gratitude for the preciousness of life. Humility is not about thinking less of ourselves, it is about thinking of ourselves less. You cannot teach someone how to be like a child; you can only suggest ways to unlearn some things in order to learn as a child would. Learning by reading is one thing; engaging your mind and body produces a different way of learning. Now let's move into a somatic practice to explore a visceral sense of beginner's mind.

BEGINNERS MIND

Begin with a deep relaxing breath, then ask yourself: What would it be like to feel a little bit more like a child? What would it feel like in my body to have that childlike sense of wonder and awe? Be the child.

- Now for a minute or two walk around with that sense of childlikeness.

- Now ask yourself: How would it feel if I felt a little like a wizened elder? What would that be like? Let your imagination run. Be an elder.

- Walk for a minute or two and explore a sense of wisdom that comes with age.

- Ask yourself: How would it feel if I felt like both a child and a wise elder at the same time?

- Take a walk as both an elder and a child combined. Notice how this feels, what do you notice in your body and in your thoughts?

What do you appreciate about these two qualities, separately and together?

Apply this practice throughout the day. If you find yourself being triggered or challenged, watch your inner life like an elderly person watches children on a playground. Feel the caring and maturity.

> Try this: The next time you are struggling with someone, imagine that the person you are struggling with is actually a wise elder or an innocent child and that you have the privilege of asking only one question to find under-standing. In this situation, you'd be sure to choose your question with reverence and great care.

Imagine what it would be like to speak to our children with this kind of rever-ence. What it would be like if our teachers, with great respect and anticipation, awaiting their answers, asked the children in their classes regularly, "What do you care about?" and "What would you love to learn today?" School would be a very different awakening experience for our children. Perhaps they would grow up with more self-awareness and cultivation of their inner compasses.

Any discipline takes vigilance in order not to fall into merely going through the motions when things are repetitive. Beginner's mind challenges us to continuously see things anew. When studying ourselves, we must engage our imagination. A beginner's curiosity invites feelings, images, senses, and vision. The master swordsman must be creative when practicing sword cuts 1,000 times a day to keep each one real and meaningful. The swordsman must cultivate the intention to correct and improve each cut. Never wrong, always better. Slowing it down to make it understandable, practicing, correcting, and practicing again. Each cut is made with the curiosity of a child and the appreciation of an elder who knows with confidence the value of intentional, deliberate, rigorous and committed practice over time.

Human beings are hard-wired to resist change and to preserve the status quo. To get over the initial hump when learning new skills it helps to anticipate resistance. Over time, intentional practice inevitably brings us face to face with old, ingrained habits and behaviors, hidden fears, and emotions. It's not a matter of *whether* we will feel resistant or stuck, but *when*. On any path of real change, the excuses we make for not continuing will become overwhelming as old hab-its fight to maintain their hold. Resistance to change can show up as tiredness, boredom, physical pain, frustration, tension, or daydreaming. So, when you tell yourself, "this weather is too nasty to train in," re-frame your thought and say to yourself: "Training in this weather will help me embrace adversity. It is fine weather to build my endurance." When you fear you can go no further, re-frame your rapidly beating heart as inner applause that appreciates how far you've come and is encouraging you onward. How you frame your experiences changes your mood and perceptions. When we choose to suspend old reactions for the sake of learning, training brings personal awakening

A Place to Wake Up

"Build it and they will come" was the prophetic message in the movie *Field of Dreams*. A practice space imbued with intention helps manifest that intention. Whether you are alone or among others, an intentional training space that feels safe and congruent with the qualities you are training to develop can significantly enhance practice in unforeseen ways. Whether you are setting a beautiful table for a special meal, in a training hall, or finding a quiet space for meditation, when creating a physical space for your personal practices, make it inviting. Do not clutter it. Orient the space so there is a front and a back. Bring into the space what feels right. Keep it clean, and wherever possible, invite a sense of the sacred. Be as intentional as possible about all aspects of it. Enter and leave it with gratitude and reverence.

A dojo can serve as a model for setting up your own training space. Dojos are traditional Japanese training halls where mastery of a chosen path is pursued. *Dojo* literally means a "place to wake up" or a "place of the way." Traditionally, the martial arts dojo was a place where the Samurai of ancient Japan could hone his spirit through the arts of conflict. In the dojo, training was grounded in codes of ethics that pertained to the protection of their community and connection with nature. There are dojos in Japan for many disciplines, from flower arranging to Zen meditation, calligraphy to the martial arts. Dojos come in all shapes and sizes.

The first Aikido dojo I opened was at a rec center with a few old wrestling mats and florescent lights in a bare room. I added some flowers and a candle, declared an intention, and we were good to go. My Aikido teacher's dojo is the Tsubaki Grand Shrine of America, the main Shinto shrine of the United States, set deep in a remote mountain river valley. Whether it is a modified garage or a magnificent shrine with live deities, it is the intention with which you imbue the training space that enlivens and empowers the practices.

We practice innumerable unconscious habits and patterns that make up the web of who we are. What we consciously choose to practice adds up to only a small part of each day. Whether your practices are lofty—such as playing the piano, meditation, or gourmet cooking—or seemingly mundane—such as making morning coffee or driving to work, the intention and the manner in which the practices are conducted makes a difference.

Alone or with others, in a kitchen, or in a grand shrine, an intentional place of training becomes a metaphor for your inner life and a microcosm for all relationships. In the dojo, you practice relaxing and staying present within gradually intensifying practice. In it, how you treat and judge others reveals a great deal about how you treat and judge yourself. Anyone can declare a dojo. The following are guidelines for declaring a training space. I invite you to use them as a springboard for creating your own criteria.

Dojo Guidelines and Intentions

- Enter the training space as a metaphor for your inner world.
- Allow time.
- Muster your curiosity.
- You are always free to begin again.
- Leave self-condemnation at the door.
- Make room for improvement and do your best.
- Practice staying present to what is alive in you.
- Train with the values you wish to embody.
- Cultivate a spirit that honors all life.
- Forgiveness is always available.
- Give your judgments only the light of your attention.

Remember: You cannot do anything wrong in the dojo and you can always do it better, so do your best.

When you find you have a response–trust it.
It has meaning.

William Stafford

CHAPTER THREE

The Seven C's of Empathic Communication

The Seven Cs—courage, curiosity, commitment, caring, center, confidence, and creativity—are elemental qualities that support the kind of practice that leads to embodiment of specific skills. Virtuous qualities that we cultivate represent a forward movement of our spirit, and by moving toward them, we embrace life.

The S.U.R.F. Centering practice in Chapter 1 offers a means to cultivate qualities such as the Seven Cs across mind, body, and spirit and over time to develop the ability to transmit those qualities through your actions, words, and presence.

Whether your aim is to become a martial artist, a masterful goldsmith, a healer, a scientist, or to simply live in greater communion with others, these seven qualities provide a means to navigate the unknowns encountered on any true path. Although we never know where things may end up, with the Seven Cs, you are at the tiller and will have what is needed to navigate the journey.

Empathy in Action

In 2008, I traveled to Awassa, Ethiopia, to offer Aikido training to Tesfaye Tukulu, a very talented martial arts instructor. A year earlier, he had come to Cypress for "Training Across Borders," an event organized through Aiki Extensions, an organization that brings the harmonizing ways of Aikido off the mat and into the world. This event brought Israeli and Arab martial artists from across the Middle East to train together in the peaceful art of Aikido.

Tesfaye's gentle, powerful, and respectful demeanor drew the attention of several of the seasoned teachers presenting there. Aikido ignited Tes, and after the summit, he immediately began Aikido training in earnest and soon opened the first Aikido dojo in Ethiopia.

The first night after we landed in Awassa, Tes and a few of the other organizers took us out on the town. After some goat tibs and charose (spice beans) and njira (Ethiopian flat bread), we went to a bar to dance. We danced into the night, tasting some of the local drink and having a lot of fun. At one point, out of the corner of my eye, I noticed Tes quietly escort two of the women who were with us out of the bar. In close pursuit was a very large, muscular man. Something didn't feel right to me, so I followed them at a discrete distance. Tes ushered the two women into a taxi, and as he turned around, he faced this angry man. I could not understand what was being said, but the tone and posture of the man was clearly confrontational. Later, Tes translated what had transpired into En- glish for me.

The man started to accuse Tes of getting in the way of his advances toward one of the women. Clearly trying to provoke a fight, his voice grew louder as he took off his shirt to expose his rippling, muscled chest and six-pack abs. Watching this spectacle, my heart began to race. I had studied martial arts for 30 years at the time, and reflexively began to ready myself if I was needed. Tes, surprisingly calm, looked at him and said with genuine curiosity: " Wow! You are really built. Where do you work out?"

The angry man, dumbfounded and caught off guard, said, "What?"

Tes replied with appreciation: "I was wondering where you work out. You're in incredible shape, and I am looking for a new gym to work out in."

At that point, the man's demeanor began to soften as he responded to Tes's interest in something he clearly valued himself. The tone of the interaction relaxed as the subject changed to workout regimes. I went back into the bar. When Tes came back in, I asked him what was going on, to which he replied amicably: "Oh, nothing. I was just talking to a new friend." I love this story because it is an example of how an empathic presence can effectively turn conflict into connection.

Tragically, one of the rarest commodities in our culture is empathy. We are hungry for empathy, and generally don't know how to ask for it. When someone needs empathy most, they often speak in a way that they are least likely to receive it. The Seven Cs are basic ingredients for training our empathic presence. In a moment of impending conflict in an amped-up situation, or when offering empathy to a friend, the basics are the same. Tes was genuinely curious about who he was talking to. He had the courage to face this man and his own fears. Tes did not take the man's words or anger personally. He was centered and able to fully listen. He had trained well and, with confidence, allowed his embodied learning to lead.

Care

To live a meaningful life, it's essential to know what you deeply care about. To deeply listen to someone with care is one of the most healing and powerfully disarming things we can do. When someone truly sees us, and in a caring way urges us into the gentleness of their attention, we leave the loneliness and dark- ness in which we have taken asylum and come into the light.

My wife Judith once told me a story that is an extreme example of this. A friend of hers was hitchhiking and got picked up by a man who proceeded to take her off the road and forced her to take off her clothes. When he climbed on top of her, she described what she felt as a deep compassion for him and the kind of pain he must be in to do such a thing. She put her arms around him and looked him right in the eyes with profound care. She said to him that he really didn't want to do what he was doing—that he wouldn't want to live with that weight in his heart. He got up, helped her back to the car, and took her where she wanted to go.

There is a quality of care that can change lives, and the principle is appli- cable daily under much less extreme circumstances. Care is an expression of connection that recognizes that to harm another is to harm one's self. The better we appreciate what each of us care about, the more readily and deeply we can connect to what is needed in the moment.

Lucricia was an elderly woman with whom I taught NVC in prisons through the Freedom Project of Seattle. Throughout the weekend-long trainings, she often remained very quiet. Her caring presence spoke volumes, and when she did speak, everyone listened. During one workshop, an inmate shared his deep wish to be less violent in his ways of interacting and worried that he would not be able to remember the lessons of NVC. Lucricia looked at him with great care and said, "Don't worry, just remember that when you speak from the heart, there is never any waste."

Curiosity

I asked my eight-year-old neighbor what curiosity is, and she replied, " Curiosity makes you want to learn about it."

Curiosity is that compelling, infectious quality that urges us to want to know, to ask questions and search for answers. When you are curious about something, your mind is observant of information and awaits new ideas related to it. The key element of "beginner's mind" is a curiosity that looks beneath the surface to discover new worlds and possibilities hidden beneath the surface of normal life. The mental exercise of curiosity habituates your mind to be open to seeking. Curiosity is not forceful; it's a vulnerable state. When someone is truly vulnerable, it is disarming. We've heard the cliché that each of us are universes unto ourselves. This being the case, how much can we truly know one another? Albert Einstein stated, *"The important thing is not to stop questioning... Never lose a holy curiosity."* Holy curiosity leads to holy connection, which happens when someone is truly listening beneath our words and actions for that sacred place within each of us that we all share. Bruce Cockburn in his Love Song said it beautifully, *"In the place my wonder comes from, there, I find you."*

When curiosity is expressed through compassion, we feel connected. When someone is genuinely curious about who we are, it feels good and moves us to share our stories.

> *A grounded touch and a listening face.*
> *When I am lost, your smile I trace.*
> *Back to the source to change my disposition,*
> *Right on course with my heart I listen.*
> *Listening to the Nature and the nature of me*
> *Igniting my soul with curiosity,*
> *It's that and that alone,*
> *something that I yearn to learn,*
> *Burning to know what's around the next turn.*
> ~ D.K.W.

COURAGE

The root of the word courage is *cor*—the Latin word for heart. In one of its earliest forms, *courage* meant "To speak one's mind by telling all of one's heart."

We all seek the experience of being connected and alive. The difficulty is that to find the connection we desire, we must not be afraid of it. Courage is not as much about going off to fight dragons as it is about facing our demons, tolerating our feelings, and not reacting so quickly, in order to hear what our emotions are trying to tell us. Empathy requires a profound fearlessness to listen to and even embrace what we do not know, sometimes for a long time. Sometimes it takes great courage to not *do* anything and just listen.

Carl Rogers, the founder of humanistic psychology, said, "What we are most ashamed of is often what is most common." We're wired to tell our stories, and even though our mother culture teaches us not to reveal our imperfections, this is where we can deeply connect. Through the years in my workshops, there is nothing more moving than when someone who is afraid to reveal his or her self musters the courage to speak out and does so for the sake of genuinely connecting and contributing to the others in the room. When someone courageously risks vulnerability against all his or her imperfections, it opens the hearts of those near by.

One day a young woman in her mid-20s, Joanne, showed up at our door. She was strung out, suicidal, and wanted help to kick her heroin addiction. Judith and I knew her half a dozen years earlier as a bright, loving, and capable friend. Now, with her mind and body compromised by drugs, she was fighting for her life.

Joanne spent the next month at our house. Never completely clean, her ability to be honest with herself was patchy. Several neighbors helped where they could, but none of us had much experience with this sort of thing. We called on our friend Peter, a former addict, now clean for 30 years, who surely had some understanding of what Joanne was up against.

Peter wept as he told us of people he had known, befriended and tried to help, who had died. He was afraid of putting his heart on the line again with someone who might go back on the streets and self-destruct. Still, he offered to go with Joanne to Narcotics Anonymous every day for the next 30 days if she would commit to it. He cared. Her courage to fight moved him; his courage to help moved her.

When last we spoke, Joanne was on a healing path. Peter died recently, and the greatest gift he left me is the courage he displayed in authentically being his caring, playful, jokester, artist self. Surprisingly, people who are considered the least likely leaders can end up inspiring us the most. Everyday people and everyday acts of courage and heart can change everything.

Center

Center is the eye of the hurricane, the place where you are able to be calm in the midst of the spinning without spinning yourself. Wisdom stories tell of the hero or prince who, when lost in the dark, lets go of the reins so his horse can lead him home. Letting go of what we think we should do and instead following our bodies' messages puts us into the truth of the present moment and allows our intuitive knowing to lead us back to center.

It is important to appreciate our histories, but lingering too long in thoughts of the past is moving backward. Similarly, it is important to do what we can to manage our future mental apparitions—thoughts that project us into imaginary future situations can create worry and fear. Balancing the anxiety and high-paced activities in our lives with stillness and provide the calm and clarity to discern what we need to stay on course. The intention of centering practices is not about being centered all the time. We are not built for that. It is to learn to come back to center more quickly when we notice we are off.

In my mid-20s, I worked as a custom goldsmith in a jewelry store owned by a gracious woman named Sachi. It was a perfect arrangement. I made the jewelry; she sold it. From time to time, a silversmith came to the store to sell semi-precious stones he had cut and some jewelry he crafted. One day, Sachi showed me a pair of stones he had cut and asked me whether she should buy them. On my advice, she decided not to purchase them. Later in the year, I realized at the company's Christmas party just how much my suggestion not to buy his stones had offended the silversmith. After he had a few drinks, he began to direct taunts and racial slurs my way, posturing to fight. I walked outside to calm down and took the moment to call my Aikido teacher and share how shaken I felt by the incident. His response was simply, " David, this guy really pulled you off your center."

I hung up and remembered my Aikido training. Breathing deeply, I centered myself. My mood shifted quickly; breathing helped me to move my attention from my head down into my heart and belly. There the enemy images faded as the potential conflict became something other than conflict. The silversmith came outside looking to fight. I was now able to hear below his threats, a man in pain. I just listened and mustered the care to understand his frustration. His heat dissipated. Shortly after that, his wife excused them both, and they went home.

Centering trains us to not just accept the experience of others, but to listen to the innate wisdom of the body and await our own experience in every moment. When centered, the mind is alert, with a heightened awareness of our surroundings and an uncanny ability to focus on essentials. Tapping deep into our center is an essential practice for addressing the challenges in personal relationships as well as for finding solutions to global problems. Centering opens a mindset of discovery that is willing to embrace change and in which there is no end to learning.

Creativity

Albert Einstein said: "Imagination ... is more important than knowledge. Knowledge is limited. Imagination encircles the world." Imagination, which is different from fantasy, is a fundamental faculty through which people make sense of the world, and it plays a key role in the learning process.

Communication, done artfully, is felt. We taste, smell, see, imagine, and notice in the nuances of gesture, tone, inflection, and movement that which we can never hear through words alone. Listening with your whole self is necessary to hear another's whole self. Chinese philosopher Chuang Tzu described empathy as a creative process when he said: "True empathy requires listening with your whole being. Hearing that is only in the ears is one thing. The hearing of understanding is another. But the hearing of the spirit is not limited to any one faculty, to the ear or to the mind. The whole being listens. There is then a direct grasp of what is right there before you that can never be heard with the ear or understood with the mind."

Norman, an elder master goldsmith, left an impression on my younger self as I watched him at his bench, immersed in the creation of jewelry. As an apprentice, I'd observe his mastery from a lifetime of practice that went into filing, carving, and shaping wax models of the jewelry that eventually I would cast into metal. At regular intervals he'd sit up and hold a wax design between his three fingers in front of his eyes with his pinky extended,—delicate and dignified—as would a gentleman sipping a cup of tea. He'd turn the wax ring and observe it from every perspective to see the whole picture, then refocus and lean intently once more into the work. Now, 40 years later, I am the same age he was then. With many years' experience now stored in my body, I see and feel myself moving in just the same ways, between sharp and defuse focus, from thinking to feeling—open, sensing, and awaiting inspiration to inform what is next. Think, feel, sense—head, heart, belly—again and again. This is the creative process—pulsing, integrating, and synchronizing head, heart, and belly through the faculty of imagination. After four decades of being a goldsmith, what I enjoy most is co-creating the symbols that are meaningful to my clients. Making a couple's wedding rings is always a sacred act and an intimate process. Some clients come with elaborate ideas drawn out in detail; others dream up an idea from scratch with me; and then there is everything in between. Throughout the process, I listen with care and open curiosity as I ask questions. My clients' answers are like a trail of breadcrumbs we can follow to their hearts' desire. I reflect back to them by scribbling sketches of the wisps of what I am hearing. They comment on the scribbles. I translate their sentiments, and we go back and forth until eventually the design to be made in metal and stone reveals itself. Deep listening manifests something that surprises everyone. To listen creatively in a way that "gets" what is meaningful to another is the essence of empathy.

Confidence

Once there was a martial arts teacher whose skill and prowess were renowned. One day a young man walked into his dojo to challenge him. The young man was quick and sharp and handily beat the older teacher. The story goes that the great teacher walked out of his dojo into the surrounding forest. After a short time he returned and with his usual power and grace, called the class together. After the customary bow, he began to teach that day's class.

Confidence that is embodied transmits a powerful yet calm resolve, awareness, and capacity. Confidence arises when we trust where we stand and what we have come to know. The Jedi master Yoda in the Star Wars trilogy said it this way: "No! Try not. Do! Or do not. There is no try." We lose confidence by trying to be it. Addressing intimate relationships, Joni Mitchell said, "The times you impress me the most are when you don't even try."

Competence is part of confidence, but there is a difference. We can be competent in something and not have confidence. Confidence requires another ingredient because it is not only a quality you feel, like joy or compassion, it's also how others describe what they see and feel when they are with you. Confidence is something we transmit by being it. What others see as confidence in you is your own experience of being fully yourself when you are not being self-conscious about what others think.

So what is confidence, and how can we get more of it? First of all, there's nothing more to get. Rather, there is something important to lose that gets in our way. Confidence is not merely about changing aspects of personality or building skill levels. It's about being present to what is happening and less distracted by what others may be thinking about us. *We develop confidence through the practice of focusing on the present moment, taking it as it comes, and giving it our all.*

Confidence is a physically expansive state. Insecurity is a contracted state that holds some element of fear. It's difficult, if not impossible, to be contracted and empathic simultaneously. When we're tight, it is hard to feel the nuanced feelings of intuition. It is also hard for someone else to relax and feel trust around us when we are contracted. Confusion and getting lost in relationships is unavoidable. The good news is that we gain confidence through sincere practice and experience over time.

Commitment

Commitment is what transforms a promise into reality. It is the words that speak boldly of your intentions and the actions that speak louder than the words. It is making the time when there is none. Coming through time after time after time, year after year after year. Commitment is the stuff character is made of; the power to change the face of things. It is the daily triumph of integrity over skepticism.

The Seven C's of Empathic Communication

In my late 20s, after three and a half years of traveling, I returned home to the US, deeply committed to shift my government' s nuclear weapons build up, named MAD—Mutually Assured Destruction—and end my country's support of brutal dictatorships, particularly in Latin America. As a US citizen, I felt moved to speak out. I settled in a small town in northern Washington State and started the Granite Falls Peace Council. Our small group met regularly to write a monthly newsletter, establish a sister town in the Soviet Union, put together fundraisers for organizations and initiatives we supported, participate in rallies, and build our network with other like-minded groups.

Whether working in global politics or raising a family, sometimes it is easy to feel that what we do is ineffectual because the problems seem so big. Margaret Meade famously said: "Never doubt that a small group of thoughtful committed citizens can change the world. Indeed it is the only thing that ever has." I wondered about the effectiveness of my efforts. About 20 years later, after the Granite Falls Peace Council had long faded into obscurity, a young woman came up to me and shared this:

"When I was a little girl, my mother brought me with her to some of the Granite Falls Peace Council gatherings. I stuffed envelopes and went along to rallies to end wars in Latin America. We marched with others to put an end to nuclear weapons proliferation and the environmental damage their production caused. Those experiences profoundly affected the rest of my life. More than anything else, it ignited my desire and determination to become a lawyer so that today I can and am working for social justice in the world. Thank you!"

When commitments and efforts are truly heart-centered, and we genuinely do our best, actions will manifest results that ripple out. Cultivate existing in the instant, believe that the world can change, and commit to your part of the solution.

The next chapter offers a series of somatic practices for grounding and empowering the choices we make and the commitments we declare.

Until one is committed, there is hesitancy, the chance to draw back, always ineffectiveness. Concerning all acts of initiative and creation there is one elementary truth, the ignorance of which kills countless ideas and splendid plans: that the moment one definitely commits oneself, then providence moves, too. All sorts of things occur to help one that would never otherwise have occurred. A whole stream of events issues from the decision, raising in one's favor all manner of unforeseen incidents and meetings and material assistance, which no man could have dreamed would have come his way. Whatever you can do or dream you can, begin it. Boldness has genius, power, and magic in it.

Goethe

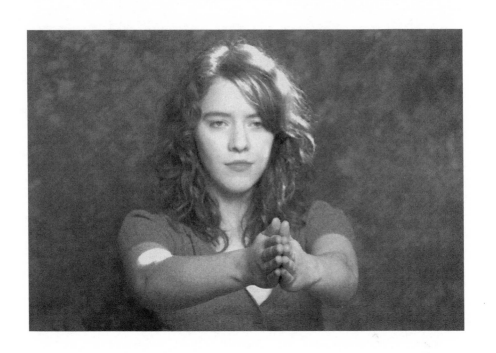

CHAPTER FOUR

Choice and Commitment

A clear and powerful commitment opens new pathways through which energy can f low. In its deepest sense, a commitment reflects the aspiration to walk a path of one's own choosing, even when it questions the life led up to that point. A well-crafted, meaningful commitment that comes from one's core illuminates the path toward one's goal. It can provide a reference in helping to determine how far one has come and the distance yet to go.

Our biological programming is wired, in part, to preserve a status quo; in other words, to gravitate toward what is familiar. Commitments that are clear and powerful help move us through our innate resistance to change. Such commitments must emerge from a deep appetite and hunger.

Initially when my family and the others started on the journey of intentional community, we really had little idea what it would entail. Our original commitment—to share resources wherever possible, to steward the land, to raise children more collaboratively, all for the sake of contributing to a more nurturing world—has endured and continues to take us far beyond what we imagined when we began. One such clear commitment within my community has been to refrain from talking negatively about others behind their backs. This came out of the painful divisiveness that resulted from careless gossip. Living out this commitment has produced more unity, more honest conversations, and a mutual respect that is tangible. We do sometimes fall back into old habits and consequently are learning the value of forgiveness and re-commitment. Nearly 30 years later, our intentional community is thriving. It has weathered intense conflict, relationship upheavals, and the disillusionment that is part of the natural cycle of community building.

Commitments that involve too much structure can hinder creativity. Conversely, too little structure can be confusing and leave us feeling directionless. Most of the free-love communes of the 1960s splintered, in part, because they lacked clear structures. Any path toward mastery begins and ends with clear commitments, structures for guidance, and doable-goals.

Commitments are weak when motivated by obligation rather than personal conviction. They are strong when entered into willingly and joyfully.

The Organizing Principle

When your thoughts are clear and you speak them out loud, they become creative actions. We create the future through language. Until you articulate a possibility in language, there is no future to move toward, no action to take, and no way for others to collaborate. When you declare a commitment to a future possibility, it is a way of making a powerful request. Of course life unfolds and moves forward regardless, but if you are consciously choosing and creating your life, a declaration serves to set a direction and galvanize intention. A conscious intention acts much like a compass bearing, setting a course and guiding you to a destination. Whether leading your own life or leading others, such commitments can become personal vision statements that work as an organizing principle for all you do.

The more grounded the declaration, the more it will galvanize resources and direction. Working somatically sets the stage for connecting with what most invigorates you. Whether your commitments are large or small, they must be tangible and doable. For example, world peace is a great idea, but it is an overwhelming goal to achieve. On the other hand, committing to meditating 20 minutes each day, journaling, or writing a newsletter to raise awareness about children involved in inner city gangs are endeavors that are doable and contribute to world peace.

In the following three practices, you don't need to make the commitment of your life. Just choose something you would love to manifest personally.

1. Shaping a Commitment
2. Resource Your Commitment (Hollow Bone Practice)
3. Empower Your Commitment (Choosing Decisively)

SHAPING A COMMITMENT

There are no greater creative words to call something forth than: " I am." As you shape a commitment for yourself find the words that speak most clearly and powerfully to you. Embodying a commitment begins by articulating it well. One suggestion to bring the commitment fully into the body is to say " I am a commitment to...." instead of " I am committed to..." Own it. Become it. Do your best to keep your commitment succinct, doable, and no more than a sentence. Be creative, have fun, and as you progress, make the language your own. Here are some suggestions to help shape and ground your commitment:

I am a commitment to_____in the greater service of_____.

I am a devotion to_____because I deeply care about_____.

I am a commitment to_____for the sake of_____.

Here are some examples:

I am a commitment to making time to sit with my wife for coffee or tea for the sake of connecting more deeply, to our happiness and well-being as a couple.

I am a devotion to practicing meditation daily in the greater service of living more gently and connectively with those I love.

I am a commitment to saving enough money to buy a new bicycle to ride regularly for the sake of having more fun and better health.

Speak your commitment aloud. Notice how it strikes you as you say it. Does it move you? Does it feel on target? What would make it truer and more powerfully engaging? Speak it again. Revise it. Speak it again. Fine-tune it. Each time you do this, you strengthen existing pathways in your brain and create and build new ones. Do it daily and the more often the better. To enhance this practice, take a physical stance that feels powerful, and pay attention to really feel what you say. (For more on this, see the Choosing Decisively practice on page 57).

Fulfilling Conditions for Your Commitments

With your commitment as the backdrop, articulate as best as you can specific tasks for manifesting your commitment:

Write down time periods for specific actions and their completion. For example, what would the criteria of success be for four months, for eight months, and for one year?

- Write down what it would look like if you were successful in completing each of these tasks.

Choose a practice partner you can designate as a listener to check in with at regular intervals over time. Help one another stay on track with your commitments.

THE HOLLOW BONE PRACTICE

The Hollow Bone Practice is a resourcing practice for replenishing one's reservoirs. One day I visited my friend Steve Old Coyote, a Native American elder, storyteller, and wood carver. While he carved a wooden staff, I asked him what he was up to. His response was, " I am thinking about what it would be like to be a hollow bone and let Spirit move through me to guide my words and actions." That is how this practice got its name. The Hollow Bone, in conjunction with the following Choosing Decisively Practice, forms one continuous practice.

A goal of training is to get out of your own way so empathic connection and intuition can arise. Keep the image in mind of being a hollow bone through which Life can flow unimpeded. Allow it to move through you with gratitude. When you have gratitude for something, you connect with it. This practice helps you remember that regardless of what you think, you are always loved, and love is always available. The Hollow Bone offers a different somatic perspective on some of the same terrain as the S.U.R.F.I.N.G. practice (page 88). The Hollow Bone brings the dynamic of postures and movement into play to spark your imagination and galvanize the learning. As you explore it, find how and where they might fit your daily life.

The Practice

1. Stand in your full length, not overextended or collapsed. With your feet slightly apart, feel the bottoms of your feet connect with the earth, and vertically align your belly with your heart and your head—a stance of dignity and grace, in line with gravity and the earth.

2. Take a deep breath in and allow any tension in your body to soften as you

exhale. Imagine opening the bottoms of your feet to the earth.

3. Take a full and relaxing breath. Imagine you are using your breath to make more space in your body while you settle into your length.

4. Bring your hands up to chest level, bending your elbows only slightly. With your fingers pointed forward, vigorously rub your hands together.

5. Move your hands apart, and extend your arms, hands, and fingers as if you were reaching out to catch a big ball. Notice the tingling of energy from the friction in your hands. Take a deep breath in and out as a way to help draw and circulate that energy.

6. Bring the warmth and the tingling fingers to your heart. Touch your heart and invite your appreciation for it.

7. Slowly begin rubbing from your heart down to your belly to connect the two. Now wake up your belly by patting it, and then bring your attention to the middle of that sensation in your belly and imagine it as a stream of energy that moves through your fingers down toward the ground.

8. Imagine sending down roots through your fingertips and through the bottoms of your feet. Imagine these roots connecting to the organisms under the soil, to the plants, the rocks, to what's above the soil, the animals, the insects, the birds, the air, the water, and the ocean. With gratitude, connect to the earth and the life of this planet. In your own way, give thanks for the nature that is all around you.

9. With fingers outstretched, turn your palms to the space behind you. As though your palms were radar dishes, use them to feel into and visualize the space behind you. Imagine that this space is like a large, soft cushion that is supporting your whole backside. Let it hold and support you, as though there are many hands holding your weight from behind. Now imagine this support coming from the ancestors you knew who were whole and healthy. Imagine this support coming from the teachers in your life who have supported you and brought you understanding and wisdom. Imagine the support coming from the great teachers in the world, the people who have inspired you, as well as the lessons that come through your own genetic history back to the beginning of time. Stand for as long as you feel inclined, sinking into this support with gratitude and appreciation.

10. Now, with your palms turned towards your body, arms extended and by

your side, move your arms about a foot to a foot and a half away from your body. Pay attention to standing in your vertical axis. Reach out as you connect to all who walk beside you—friends, peers, brothers and sisters who surround you—and in your own way, be grateful for all who walk by your side.

As a daily practice, little by little, try offering gratitude to those whom you may consider difficult to be around. They may be the ones who help you see parts of yourself that you would never see with those who are easy and comfortable to be with. I often think of someone that I have difficulty being around as a Light Bringer. This is because your relationship with them shines a light on places in you that no one else could. In Aikido, those who are the most difficult to train with are the ones we learn the most with. In your own way, give gratitude for those who walk beside you in your life.

11. With your arms still by your side, turn your palms forward to feel into the space in front of you. Think of all the young ones who you support and who will lead us into the future, who bring fresh perspective, lightness, and buoyancy to our lives, those who remind us to play and view the world with wonder and awe. Here you can think of someone specific or younger ones in general. In your own way, give gratitude for those young ones in your life.

12. Now take these resources that are under your feet, at your back, at your sides, and in front of you. Bring your arms up as if you were shaping a large chalice. Make the space between your arms big enough to hold the resources you have gathered. Imagine you are holding a giant cup or bowl that contains these resources. Imagine this cup is filled to the brim with all your relationships, human and nonhuman. With gratitude, drink until you are fully quenched.

13. Now, filled and renewed, bring your arms slightly to the front of you. With this bounty, in this open stance, you can offer and receive simultaneously. Reach out, and with your whole self offer what you have and receive what you are being given. Reach out to what is reaching toward you. Dedicate yourself to what you want to put out into the world as you replenish and renew yourself. This is the Hollow Bone practice.

Hollow Bone Nano Practice

You can make this practice as long or as short as you want. Here is the shortened version: Stand in your full length. Take a deep breath. Exhale loudly. Relax into your full length. Rub your hands together. Touch your heart. Pat your belly. Give thanks to the earth. Reach behind you and give thanks to all that supports you. Reach out to the side and give thanks to all who walk beside you. Reach to the front and give thanks to all who are in front of you. Hold your hands up, drink, offer, and receive. It takes only a few seconds to center yourself, to remember that you are never alone, that you always have access to resources, and that you can bring them through you. You always have access to your needs and can draw them up from within. Remember, life is not about being centered all the time. It's about recognizing when you are off center and being able to come back to center more quickly. With this exercise, you can revitalize yourself anytime, anywhere. To feed the practice, here are a few questions to consider:

- How was it for you?
- How did you feel before?
- How did you feel after?
- How is it to receive and offer at the same moment?

When you make note of the feelings and bodily sensations, over time they will become more familiar and you will be able to come back to that feeling more quickly. You are not alone when you choose to connect to your support.

CHOOSING DECISIVELY

Whether the decision or commitment you are considering is large or small, this practice offers direction and helps you discern whether you are on the mark or not. It uses the metaphor of a sword to indicate a powerful cutting away of what is not needed to make room for what is essential. This practice is a good place to re-frame the sword—not as something for killing, but as a tool to cut away what is unnecessary, the sharper the better. In the kitchen, my wife makes great beauty because her knives are kept sharp. The less sharp the knife, the more forceful you need to be to cut.

We prune a tree to make it healthier. Decisiveness requires the ability to cut away what does not serve our deeper needs. A relationship that is not nurturing any-one, a job that is robbing you of your health or sanity, or an attitude that is in the way of your friendships—these are things we may choose to cut away for the sake of our highest well-being. The sword represents the things what needs to die so that we may focus on what is truly valuable and life serving. The only way to work with a sword is harmoniously.

1. Center and Open to What Is Possible.

Standing, align your feet with your shoulders, head over your heart, and heart over your belly. Take a deep breath in and release, settling into your full vertical length. Relax. Open your arms and hands as if someone were handing you a large beach ball. Be curious, open, and listen with all your senses and imagination to the possibilities in this moment.

2. Pick One

Pick one decision or commitment you would like to make and are in question about. Choose some- thing specific and doable. Bring your hands in front of your belly as though you were holding that one choice and grasping a sword handle.

State your commitment or the decision you want to make as succinctly and clearly as possible.

Make it meaningful by grounding it in what you care about.

For example: *"I choose to devote myself to practicing meditation daily, because when I do, I feel a greater sense of peace."* or *"I commit to take a moment each day to listen more deeply to my spouse's needs and react less for the sake of our happiness and well-being as a couple."*

Make sure your choices are doable and not overwhelming. Commitments such as "world peace" or "a new life" can be too large, hard to grasp, and discouraging, so break it down to what you can truly manage. Try the forms I am suggesting for speaking, but in time find your own ways to speak your commitments.

3. Prepare and Commit

Prepare yourself physically for a powerful sword cut. Bring your hands to just above your forehead. Thumbs point toward your forehead, and the "blade" of your hands (pinky side) faces away. Begin with your fingers pointing to the sky and elbows extended in front of you. Remember the ground that you stand on, the resources at your back, all who walk beside and those who are in front of you. As you imagine your hands forming the blade of a sword, speak your commitment or the decision you are trying to make. Speak from your belly, and let the power grow, build, and come through you in service to all your relationships.

4. Initiate: Release Your Power

Let the power of your choice build, and then release the power. As you make the sword cut, take one step forward and let out a loud, sharp *"haaaa"* or *"yyeeess"* or *"saaaa"* that emanates from your core.

5. Enter: Accept the Consequences of your Action

Having completed the sword cut, take a step into your commitment. Stand in your dignity and grace to accept the consequences of this first step and notice how it feels and the thoughts that come up for you. Does it feel like a good choice? Does it feel strange or off in some way? How does your choice feel to you now? Do you need to make a correction? Is it a step in the right direction? Do you want to go back or turn in a different direction?

Sometimes, when you don't know what to do, it is common to get overwhelmed and feel stuck. By taking one first step, you can experience enough of the consequences to not be overwhelmed and to inform your next step.

6. Relax: Assess

Let your arms fall to your sides and take a relaxing breath. Bring your attention into the sensations in your body. Notice how it feels to have made a choice and taken this action. Listen to your body's guidance. Relax, observe, reflect, and be present with what arises within your heart, mind, and body after this practice.

As a daily practice, take notice of your habitual responses and historical strategies. Welcome and become familiar with questions that inevitably arise:

- What and who do I truly value and why?
- How do I want to show up in my life?
- Do my words and actions line up with what I believe is important?

Be Specific.

With the commitment as the backdrop, articulate and write down as best as you can:

- Specific tasks for delivering on your commitment.
- Time periods for specific actions and their completion. For example, what would the criteria of success be for four months, for eight months, and for one year?
- What it would look like if you were successful in completing each of these tasks?

Let's Review The Steps

1. Be open to choice.
2. Choose one commitment to start.
3. Articulate your commitment.
4. Initiate the commitment.
5. Enter and assess.
6. Relax.

Remember: Notice how your commitment strikes you as you say it. Does it move you? Does it feel on target? What would make it more powerfully engaging?

Build the neural pathways: Remember daily what you care about. Speak it again. Correct it. Speak it again. Repeat. Do it daily, and the more the better.

*This practice is gratefully adapted from Stuart Heller's Sword Cut Practice.

Learning is accelerated with others. Choose a practice partner you can check in with at regular intervals over time. Help one another stay on track with your commitments. With a partner or several people, you can accelerate your practice. Speak your commitment to the listeners. Notice how it feels to say it. Are you speaking from a deep place inside you? Notice how it strikes your body as you say it. Notice how it grabs the person(s)you're speaking to.

Now debrief. Ask how it struck them. Did they feel depth and passion in what you were speaking? Did they feel your intention strongly? Ask them what they noticed. Ask them how powerfully your declaration landed on them. (Use a scale of one to ten.) Most important, see if you can notice within yourself places of constriction, places where there is a deadening of sensation, places where you have a sense of fear or pain. Do it again and see if you can improve.

Keep in mind that emotional fear is often felt as physical pain. Physical pain can be produced by emotional fear, but not necessarily increased by it. It is important to learn to discern the difference. It is very difficult to connect emphatically with others when you are in pain or nervous. By declaring your commitment, both purposefully and daily, in time you can embody your intention and move it to a place of manifestation.

The wound is the place where light enters you

Rumi

CHAPTER FIVE

Core Contractive Strategies

"Better than Chocolate!"

The following is a wonderful story and practice that materialized in one of my classes of 7 to 12 year-olds. It came on the heels of a heartwarming three-day intensive training with several of their parents. After a bit of play and getting to know one another, I asked this question to the children sitting around the circle: " What do you really love?"

This kind of question is so rarely asked of us in our early years that most of us find ourselves struggling for an answer even now. But finding an answer puts us directly in touch with our deeper needs.

One of the children exclaimed, " Ice cream!" I suggested she imagine a tall building, and that if ice cream were one of the upper floors, what would be on the ground floor? Her voice softened, and a tiny bit of color came to her face as she said, " My family and our dog." I asked her to point to where in her body the center of that loving feeling was and to say how it felt. She pointed to just below the middle of her chest and said, " Nice!"

Then I walked about ten feet away, turned and faced her, and asked that she imagine I was a stranger, someone she had never met before.

From that distance, I asked, " Am I in your space now?" To which she replied, "No." If she had said, " Yes," I would have backed up until she felt relaxed and then checked with her to be sure that I was not in her space. Her task was to say "Stop" when I entered her personal space as I slowly walked toward her.

When I was about four feet away, she said, "Stop!" I asked, " Where in your body do you feel the feeling that tells you I am in your space?" These are unusual questions to ask anyone, but with a little coaching people will notice the tensions and contractions that occur somewhere in their bodies that alert them to a possible danger. She pointed to her chest and said that it felt tense.

Together, we connected the dots. *This was the same spot where she most acutely felt that feeling of love too!*

I suggested the tensing might be her own love and caring trying to get her attention to warn her so she would be safe. She agreed. I coached her to say to that place in her chest, " Thank you for warning me and caring for me." She realized that as she acknowledged that place, the tension in her chest relaxed and she felt much better.

I moved a little closer and again a slight triggering came up in her chest. I suggested that she engage that tense spot in a conversation, beginning with, "I am listening" and "What would you suggest that I do now?" She did this and, to my amazement, she simply walked around me like a passerby on the street. She then thanked this "inner voice" for the caring and guidance.

She lit up, immediately understanding the value of being able to turn inward to find clarity and council from a place that cared deeply about her safety and well being.

I asked how it felt to have this " inner friend." She exclaimed, *"It's better than chocolate!"* We high-fived.

I proceeded to do the same process (with minor variations) with each of the 10 kids in the class and had very similar experiences with each child. After class, one of the children came up to me and said: " My father works so hard. I wish he would listen to that part of himself more. I think he would be a lot happier."

Imagine how it would be to grow up cultivating such a friendship with our own bodies. In adult workshops, it's pretty clear that those "inner friends" that put us in touch with our needs have too often been ignored for a very long time. The deep pain and joy of reunion can be profound.

A Place of Grace

Each of us is born with an unencumbered place in ourselves, free from expectations, harsh judgments, regrets, humiliation, shame, ambition, distress, and fear —a place of original grace and kindness. There is a place to come home to within each of us, although we may have lost touch with it. Christian theologians call this place the soul; psychologists, the psyche; Hindus, Atman; Buddhists, the Dharma; Native Americans, Great Spirit. Jesus called it Love. In NVC, I believe this is what Marshall Rosenberg was referring to when he spoke of our universal human needs. To know this inward place is to know ourselves not by the surface masks of identity we have taken on, not by our occupation or clothing styles, but by feeling our relation to this inward place and inhabiting it.

Refining your self and becoming who you want to be is a process of first recognizing the constant layering over of our beginnings, and then chipping away the nonessentials—the parts that no longer serve us. Any path toward mastery requires a lifelong commitment to peel back these layers and our self-limiting beliefs while seeking peace and guidance from that incorruptible, inward place of grace at our core, no matter what it takes. While self-discovery—recovering access to that place of inner peace and self-acceptance—takes work and can be unsettling, it is a homecoming that is well worth the effort. Taking time for communion with our deepest knowing is essential, because in our depths we are all beautiful. As we discover this, healing, connection, empowerment, and community emerge.

By paying attention to our bodies' emotions, sensations, and the stories we tell ourselves, we can trace habitual patterns embedded in our nervous system back to their origins. By becoming familiar with old reactions and appreciating when, how, why, and where these historical, unconscious strategies show up, they become compost for developing new, more inclusive and collaborative responses to conflict and resistance. By noticing where our muscles tighten, how our breathing changes, and where our contractions are, we can touch those precious parts of ourselves that we've learned to protect. Then, with care, attention, and practice, it becomes possible to transform old reactions into new resources that are life enriching. This is the realm of Somatics in bodywork, personal practices, and coaching.

As living organisms, humans are wired for contact. In moments when we meet, boundaries touch boundaries, actions trigger reactions, and beneath the words we use and the stories we tell ourselves, there is a play of nonverbal forces, habits, and responses. What we communicate through tone, gesture, and movement exceeds the impact of our choice of words.

A rush of energy happens in response to any challenge, large or small—from being held at gunpoint to the ringing of the telephone. This rush of energy represents the force of change we feel in response to either internal or external stimulus. When we're startled, our system is flooded with a stream of energy to prepare us to react to the perceived threat and restore familiar ground.

When the demands of life exceed our inner resources — just as the iris of the eye contracts to regulate how much light we take in —our bodies contract to regulate the intensity of emotional experiences. This is to ensure that we remain within the limits of what we can handle. I call the deeply embedded physical, emotional, and linguistic patterns of behavior we have historically put in place to regulate the amount of energy we can tolerate *core contractive strategies*. During intense upsets, when we feel overwhelmed, our resistance to the increased energy we experience can knock our systems out of alignment. We "check out" of the situation, throttle down the energy that is streaming through us, and adopt familiar, conditioned, habitual behaviors. Bruce Lee, one of the foremost martial artists in the world, put it this way: "*Under duress, we do not rise to our highest expectations, we fall back to what we have practiced most.*"

Core contractive strategies can show up anywhere in the body, often around the face, head, eyes, shoulders, gut, chest, jaw, legs, back, and sphincter muscles. Core contractions originate in defining moments and over time from trauma or recurring themes that have impacted us, such as the loss of a parent, a divorce, being left alone for extended periods, the addition of a new sibling, an abusive relationship, even the backfiring of a car at the wrong time for an unsuspecting child. If not fully processed when they originally occur, such experiences congeal in the body and, through repetition, become a part of how we literally shape ourselves. Each contraction, like the pain when you get a cut, is a signal from your body informing you to attend to something vital. Embodied historical narratives and automatic habits that we suppress or ignore eventually taint our clarity and expression and can compel our actions beyond what we may intend or desire.

Learning to appreciate and hold the quirky, somewhat neurotic behaviors that we each have, instead of always being held by them, requires building a friendship with ourselves. When our reactions are not in sync with our words, those listening to us get mixed messages. For clarity in our communication, it's essential to be aware of the physical, nonverbal reactions we feel and transmit. New insights and less suffering become available when we pay attention to what resides in the body, investigate it, and in time learn to understand it. Power can be found in our uniqueness. Our insecurities are a doorway to our soul. They ask us to go deeper to understand ourselves and feel peace. When we feel shame or humiliation about ourselves, we transmit an energy that amplifies our insecurities. When we embrace our unique oddness, it starts to work for us, to eventually become our signature and our power.

LOCATING YOUR CORE STRATEGIES

Set-Up: A Partner Practice

This practice is most easily done with a partner; however, it also can be done alone by imagining another person and moving slowly through the steps. There are two roles in this practice:

ï   The "Receiver" is the person being triggered.

ï   The "Challenger" is someone walking toward the Receiver and represents an unknown presence, someone who may or may not pose a threat.

Going directly to the body can evoke historical reactions. For some people, this can be startling and potentially re-traumatizing, so be mindful, pay attention, and take care to notice any overwhelming responses when working with each other's personal space. In this role-play, on a scale of 1-10, keep the Challenger's perturbing role at a 2 or 3

Begin:

1. Challenger: Stand on the far side of the room opposite the Receiver, 6-10 feet away and outside the Receiver's personal space. Very slowly begin to walk directly toward the Receiver. Note that each of us has an appropriate distance for self-protection, and it varies from person to person. Our physical responses to another's proximity are the emotional alerts that remind us to pay attention for our own safety.

2. Receiver: As with the children at the beginning of this chapter, imagine the challenger walking toward you as an unknown presence. As the Challenger moves toward you, the moment you sense that the Challenger is just at the edge and stepping into your personal space, say, "Stop." Once the Challenger stops, scan your body for any tension you feel in response to this "potential threat." What is going on inside your body that tells you someone is now in your space?

Where is there a sense of discomfort or contraction in your body? Where is the feeling most acute? *This is your core contraction.*

3. Receiver: As you bring your attention into the sensations you feel in your body, see if you can find the epicenter of the tension and sensations you feel.

- Notice what you feel.
- Notice how it feels.
- Notice where you feel it. Point to it.
- Breathe into it. Gently let your breath begin to loosen the contraction.

4. Debrief

5. Switch Roles

In this practice, look for historical patterns as they show up in the body. Take care when doing this with others, as it can re-stimulate old traumas. If you find it difficult to notice your own contractive responses, the Challenger may have to get creative and amp up the trigger a little more, repeatedly approaching in different ways to initiate a response. On the other hand, sometimes the Receiver's response is so overwhelming that a specific contraction cannot be identified because it gets lost in an overall body response. I have encountered several people who will say " stop" when I am 20 to 30 feet away because I have already triggered an overwhelming response in them. In situations like these, the Challenger can begin much farther away, then approach more slowly so that the Receiver can feel the very first initial response before becoming overwhelmed.

In several of these role plays, I have had to go out the door and 30 feet from the house where I was viewed through the window so the person I was working with was able to not have an overwhelming response before I began walking in his or her direction. This practice can have many potential outcomes. Exaggerated distances like this indicate a deep sensitivity and extreme protective mechanisms, usually connected to a past trauma. The distances are different for everyone, occasionally very surprising, and always informative. There are no wrong answers.

Stay curious. Once at an NVC training in Monroe Prison, an inmate I worked with could not feel or locate a contraction or sense of discomfort in his body as I entered his space; however, the moment I turned to walk away from him, to our surprise, this stirred an emotional pain in him and old stories of abandonment.

Some part(s) of the Receiver's body will show a physical contraction, discomfort or even lifelessness. If the Receiver does not say "stop," keep bringing attention back to the actual sensations in his/her body, and make sure the Receiver is actively imagining the Challenger as an unknown presence. The Challenger can help by watching the Receiver closely to help point out where the Receiver contracts or shows discomfort.

Core Strategies

Befriend yourself. When we default to our core contractive responses, we utilize more of our implicit (preverbal) memory responses. Our reptilian brain kicks in, and as we shift to our sympathetic nervous system, some of our higher reasoning power becomes difficult or even impossible to access. This natural rush of energy and our fight/flight responses make sense if we imagine how our early ancestors lived in the wild. Rapidly accessed, intuitive, automatic responses were essential when danger approached: gathering themselves to meet the threat quickly and powerfully, tensing their legs to go into a crouch, quieting their breath to listen, focusing their eyes. After an intense encounter, they might walk for miles back to their tribe, trembling and crying to process the trauma's residual energies and allow their systems to recalibrate as they were made to do. In our modern culture, all too often this gathering of energies and processing of residual tension gets detoured, tamped down, and blocked as we conform to acceptable cultural norms. We struggle for survival to pay the bills; there are wars and daily violence on the news. We are told to sit quietly, be a good girl, boys don't cry, and to do what we are told—even when it goes against our own heart's advice or our gut instinct. In this way, that same energy that gathers to meet a threat, that once naturally got processed, is instead stopped up and left unreleased. Unreleased energy manifests in our bodies as chronic low-grade tension in our shoulders, headaches, back problems, shallow breathing, and narrow focus. Most of us live with some form of subconscious, unprocessed trauma all the time.

You cannot lose your history. Historical strategies, developed out of need and then practiced for years, don't go away. As you grow and change, some of the old strategies can hinder you. Learning to honor the truth that when you were younger, these were the best strategies you could come up with, is the key to getting in touch with hidden and preciously protected parts of yourself. Learning to catch your triggered responses more rapidly and work with them instead of against them is a profoundly transformative practice.

Now let's repeat the approach of this unknown presence. This time, notice which of the following is most familiar to you:

- Do you want to fight or flee?
- Do you want to connect?
- Do you want to sever connection and create boundaries?
- Do you freeze, appease, or go limp?

When our " fight/flight/submit" strategies kick in, we switch to our default modes and assume specific historical posture, speech, and gestural patterns; breathe a certain way; and take a stance, literally, that manifests the tendency. Some people will habitually demure or acquiesce, while others are quickly moved to anger. Some are compelled to help, while still others tune out or focus narrowly on themselves. Core contractions and strategies form at any time in our lives, but most profoundly during early development when our brains and bodies are in rapid change. In our early years, we live within questions such as, "What will keep me safe and bring me love?" We attempt to create strategies for securing safety and love that all too often sound something like: " If I do what they want me to do, I will be loved?" or " If I keep my opinions to myself, I will be safe?"

My mother in-law, Patricia, once said to me that a child's world is like being in a room with the doorknob only on the outside. Such circumstances create unique strategies. One example of this is our cultural response to toddlers who naturally live by two directives: to explore the world and to stay safe near their parents or caregivers. Approximately every nine minutes, a toddler is told to "stop that" or "don't do something." These directives are compounded when the additional threat of "or else" is applied. This sets up a double bind for the child between exploring and being safe—a distressing conflict between the freedom and the nurturing needed at that time of life. This is one example of the cultural norms that embed a lifelong pattern of low-grade fight/flight strategies into our system. At a very early age, it is not only confusing, it can be damaging. Charles Darwin surmised that habit, repeated long enough, becomes encoded in our genes and memory. Not only do we do this with our children, it was done to us. Aspects of these strategies that we develop and employ in our childhoods can become inappropriate or ineffectual as adults. A demanding "Don't!" sends a conflicting message at any age. Asking someone to do a "don't" is confusing because it does not offer a specific request for what to do.

Don't

Please don't hurt your little brother! Don't interrupt me when I am talking.

Clear and doable requests:

Please speak in a gentler tone when you are working things out with your little brother. Please let me finish what I am saying; then I would love to hear what you want to share.

Ask for what you want in clear, doable language; not for what you don't want.

WORKING WITH YOUR CORE STRATEGIES

1. Receiver: When you feel the tension and contraction in your body, as yourself, "Where in my body do I feel a tightening or contraction or any other sensation that warns me of someone being too close?"

- Notice what you feel.
- Notice how it feels
- Notice where you feel it.

2. Breathe into the core contraction, give it the light of your attention, and let your breathing slowly soften it. This contraction is something you learned to do at some early, often traumatic point in your life and have practiced ever since. Sense whether this contraction feels old or familiar, and then ask yourself:

- Is it in my best interest to go to the source of this contraction? In other words, ask this tender place if it would be willing to have a conversation with you and then await an answer. If you have a positive response to your inquiry then move to the following questions:

- "How old was I when I learned this?"

Don't think about your answer. Let it come. Notice your first thought. If there is not an immediate answer or one is not accessible, ask the question again and note your first uncensored thought that comes to mind. Was it when you were born or age 3, 5,10, or 27? There is no wrong answer. Your first guess is often your best guess.

- Once you have identified an age, ask yourself, "What was going on in my life when I first learned that strategy?" For example: parents were divorcing, older sibling was a bully, I was made fun of at school, abuse by a family member, we moved and I felt lost, etc.

Engage your imagination and stay open to the notion of the body as a met- aphor. Employ your creativity and guess what this contraction in your body was originally in service to. Listen creatively and watch with an intuitive sense trained on what is unfolding, and be willing to be surprised. There is not a right or wrong answer to these kinds of inquiries. Find appreciation for the deeper needs under the core contractive strategy, take some time to appreciate the importance and beauty of this precious part of you that you have protected   by contracting around for so long.

- Contractions around the chest could be to protect your heart from heart-break and protect your ability to love.

- Tightness in the throat may be a metaphor for holding back your self-expression. Contractions around the throat and the mouth could be a strategy for safety or belonging by quieting and not expressing yourself.

- Contraction around your belly could be to protect and preserve your own instincts and intuition if they were not being appreciated or respected by those around you.

- Contractions around your legs or feet might be about running away or stepping forward to fight as a strategy for safety.

- Your head might hurt as a strategy to remind you to stop thinking, to keep your thoughts quiet and to yourself in order to be loved or safer.

- Tightness in your back may point to the "support" you missed from someone at your back, such as a parents or an elder.

As you identify the precious needs under the strategies, translate negative lan- guage such as, "not wanting to appear stupid" into positive language such as the "need for self respect."

Holding that younger part of yourself, the newborn, 5, 12 or 20-year-old, value how he or she has been and still is working tenaciously for your welfare. Every core contraction is a message for you to listen into. The less you listen to it, the more it will try to get your attention. Try not to judge that younger self's strategies. Just appreciate the intent behind the strategies you have developed to keep you safe and loved. Note that because you are here, safe and present to be reading this page, somehow those old strategies worked! Take some time to appreciate the importance of these precious parts of yourself that you protect and (contract around.)

- With only that in mind, gently say "thank you" to the younger you for working so diligently for your welfare.
- Notice and be with the emotions that arise.
- How is it for you to appreciate this younger part of yourself?

  * It may be difficult to appreciate and not judge that younger self. If that is the case, it may take some time, care, and patience. For now, start by appreciating the intention of this younger part of you a little at a time. The greater the pain, the more empathy and time will most likely be needed.

- Whenever the Receiver feels complete with the exercise, debrief and then switch roles.

Everyone has default patterns as unique as a fingerprint, created to protect some aspect of their core being and for keeping the world manageable. And because this becomes a part of our identity, naturally we catch ourselves defending our self-contractions. In a triggered state, trying to be empathic with each other or with ourselves becomes almost impossible because empathy is a physically expansive, not a contracted state. We can learn to notice when we have been knocked off center, so that we can more quickly settle our systems and come back to center.

One of my clients, Bill, came to me with a dilemma. He said that although he saw himself as a good communicator, when someone confronted him with anger or an accusation, he would lose his train of thought, become defensive, and compulsively retaliate. Only later would he be able to think back on what it was that he would have rather said. I asked him to imagine the last time this occurred and what was being said to him when he first felt triggered. He explained that one of the women in his community had accused him of conspiring and collud- ing with others against her. He knew in his heart of hearts that this was untrue, but he lost his temper. He knew it would be better if he had listened to find some understanding, then spoken his own truth. Instead, he angrily denied her allegations and only later, long after the conversation, wished he had been more compassionate and effective in the ways he knew how to be.

Bill and I set up a role-play, and as we reran that triggering moment, he felt his chest tighten. We brought his attention to this core contraction and with care asked, "How old were you here when you first learned to tighten your chest like that?" The immediate hit was 12. We began a very slow, gentle conversation with 12-year-old Billy.

Bill asked Billy: "What is it that you are wanting me to hear? Are you worried and trying to warn me about something?" Billy responded with, "I'm afraid

Mary will not listen, so I have to speak loudly and angrily to get her to hear me." Bill gave a long pause to let that sink in as he appreciated how this strategy was so important to his younger self. Bill replied genuinely: "Thank you for letting me know that. I really hear how you want to be listened to, especially when someone is accusing you of something you know you did not do." And then Bill added: "That must be especially painful when, in the past, you had not been listened to well. Is that right?" He felt Billy (his own chest) relax, and after a moment, went on.

Bill allowed lots of space to take it all in. In time, Bill respectfully told Billy: "Whenever I push back hard like I did with Mary, there is always some mess I have to clean up afterward. I think there are ways we can be more effective if you and I work together." Billy seemed to agree. Bill asked if Billy would be up for hearing a strategy that might help them both be heard and understood better. Billy was. "I suggest that when you sense trouble, please continue to warn me by tensing my chest. Instead of ignoring you, I will strive to listen to your concerns. Then together, let's assess the danger and decide whether it is best to speak up immediately, or if it would be better to first listen, try to understand what the other person needs, and then you and I speak our truth as one voice. I think we might be understood and get our message across better that way. What do you think?"

Billy was quiet for a moment and then agreed this might be worth a try and that this felt like a good starting place. Sometimes these smallest moments of connection produce the greatest results. Bill was earnest in his personal practice. Through the S.U.R.F.I.N.G. and Hollow Bone practices, he spent time building trust and understanding in his relationship with Billy. The next few times he felt challenged, he fumbled, and it took a while to come back to his and Billy's agreement. But very slowly, over time, they began to speak more and more as a unified self.

Centering

There are things we can change and things we cannot. It is up to each of us to discern what is possible and what is not. Recent studies of the brain's neuroplasticity show that, contrary to old myths, old dogs can learn new tricks. Through our biological evolution, we are hard-wired to maintain a status quo. Among the breakdowns and breakthroughs that are part of developing new habits are two reactions: one is a kind of panic about letting go of control because we identify with the old familiar strategies; the other is a sense of aliveness and possibility as we begin to reorganize, frame things differently, and find deeper meaning in what we are becoming. This is where centering practices come in.

Viktor E. Frankl, a concentration camp survivor and humanitarian said: "Between stimulus and response there is a space. In that space is our power to choose our response. In our response lies our growth and our freedom." Over time, through employing centering and re-centering practices in various situations, it's possible to lengthen the time between the stimulus and the automatic default response by a fraction of a second. This crucial moment provides enough space to consciously shift our strategies to more effective and inclusive ways to respond to pressure and conflict in our relationships.

When centered, we can feel our emotions. When un-centered, the tendency is to operate more mechanically through old, established, well-practiced patterns of comporting and expressing ourselves. Centering establishes awareness around our emotions, which allows them to be felt so we can notice where we feel it, where we hold our hurt and pain, and what it is trying to say to us. In this way, our bodies' signals become an "inner guidance system" to warn us of danger and bring direction and clarity to the choices at hand.

A SETTLING PRACTICE

Here is excellent practice for calming body and mind when a fight/flight state arises or as a daily centering practice. This practice relaxes our systems enough to discern whether any danger perceived is present and real or historically triggered and can be managed differently now. This discernment makes space for more effective and empathic responses. Use it whenever you find yourself feeling anxious or stressed to "reset" your system.

Practice

1. Begin by standing tall in your full length, not overextended or collapsed, and with your feet slightly apart. Feel the bottoms of your feet connect with the earth. Vertically line up your belly with your heart with your head, and center them between your feet.

2. Bend at your knees and touch the earth with the tips of your fingers. Bring to this moment a sense of gratitude for the ground that supports you and connects you to nature's bountiful resources.

3. As you come to standing, bring your hands up your centerline, starting at your belly, palms facing away from each other, fingers pointing down and hands not touching each other. As your hands reach chest level, slowly go up on the balls of your feet and breathe in deeply as your hands continue to rise above your head.

4. Imagine your hands like the water from a spring, coming from the ground

through you and refreshing you. As your hands move above your head, let them stream out as you turn your palms outward, away from each other, with fingers extending.

5. Now let your arms and hands slowly come down like the downward stroke of a wing. Begin releasing your breath.

6. As you settle, imagine that your weight is nested in your belly and that gravity is anchoring you to the ground from your belly. Allow your arms to feel this weight as well.

7. Once your arms are down, look to the left, then to the right, then behind you to the left and the right, and then above you all around. Do you see any real danger?

8. This cognitive assurance that there is no real danger or threat helps quiet the fight/flight response and relaxes the contractions in your body.

Feed the practice by asking: What do you notice in your body after having completed this practice? What feels different? What are some circumstances in your life that you encounter on a regular basis where this practice could help?

An additional visualization

Take a deep breath in and bring your arms up. Slowly let out a long, even breath as you gradually bring your hands down from up high to touch the earth. As your hands come down, imagine yourself as a coffee press, gathering and pressing the coffee grounds down through the water. Imagine this press moving from the top of your head, gathering and moving any muck that you've picked up and are holding in your thoughts, heart, belly, and throughout your body, down to your toes, and with the last bit of breath, exhale and push this mass you've gathered below your feet, deep into the molten center of the earth to burn up.

Now as you slowly breathe in, imagine you are a tree. Drink in the nutrients from the soil, and as you come back to standing, raise your arms, imagine branches extending, leaves opening from your belly, heart, lungs, and head to catch the light from the sun. Repeat, and then look around to make sure there is no danger, and relax.

Re-framing our Narratives

Invariably, we all grow up creating strategies that organize around a unique set of circumstances. The experiences and stories we carry settle, through repetition and practice, into our muscles, cells, intentions, and what we communicate. These contractions, embedded stories, and their strategies are hard to change. Responses originating in past experiences can cloud more effective responses in the present moment.

By paying attention to the narratives we've embodied, it is possible to side step the stories that spin around and around in our heads. Our reactions make visible what is embedded in our nervous systems. By tracing our habitual patterns back to their source, it becomes possible to assess their efficacy and then adjust and improve our strategies. Emotions are messengers that inform our choices. Whether a threat is real or imagined, the emotional pain we feel as our bodies tense and contract tells us there is something that needs or at least asks for our attention. Contracting around emotional pain dampens the pain and shields us from re-stimulation. It also keeps us from fully engaging the core resources within us that we are protecting. We tuck away our most precious assets, distancing ourselves from our bodies' important messages. These messages, if chronically ignored, become a source of disease. When listened to, these messages can lead toward greater self-acceptance and awareness of our personal power and unique gifts.

Core contractions and strategies have their place. The meaning, interpretations, and narratives we assign fortify them. When we experience beauty, a gorgeous sunset, or a plate of delicious food, for example, a core strategy we may develop around these experiences is relaxation and a feeling of expansion. Some of us may have learned to open our hearts when someone says "I love you," whereas others, raised under different circumstances, may have learned to feel fear, mistrust, and emotional pain—contractive states of being—when they hear the same words. We become expansive when we live in the feeling of what we love and care about, and become contracted when we are in pain or fearful. Over time, such expansive and contractive strategies become unconscious, embodied, deeply embedded in our nervous system and integral parts of our unique personalities. How we shape ourselves is inextricably linked to how we shape our relationships and the world around us, as well as how the world responds back to us. What we deny becomes our destiny; what we embrace becomes our destiny.

Consciously lived, each story we hold is a potential source of wisdom. Unconsciously lived, the same narratives limit us considerably. The stories we live in reveal our uniqueness and our commonality. Sharing them can be connective and healing. Everything we see, the experiences and circumstances in each moment, weave into the unfolding stories we create. The glass can be half empty or half full.

The stories that we tell our selves can be destructive or constructive. What prescription do you want to write for yourself? What is the narrative about your living that you are creating? How would you like to re-frame your life so that its unfolding serves you in better ways?

WRITING PRACTICES

A Somatic Autobiography

This is a contemplative practice that can reveal resources for healing and compassion. Quietly writing can help you notice, reflect, and bring awareness to habits and patterns that may have served you in your past but may no longer serve you in the present.

As you write, start at the beginning, as early as you can remember and ask yourself:

- What are the significant moments and experiences throughout my life that have shaped me emotionally, physically, and psychically?

- What are the core stories and strategies (cultural, personal, familial) that have developed from these significant moments and experiences? How have they shaped my body and perceptions?

- What are some of the qualities, virtues, and moods of important people in my life that now show up in me?

- How do different aspects of my personal history and beliefs move me forward or hold me back in creating the life I desire?

As you move from the general to the specific in the telling and writing, you might ask yourself:

- When I am telling my story, what am I feeling?

- Where do I feel it in my body?

- What specific beliefs have I built around my story? (I'm not lovable. I'm not smart. I'm a dreamer.) Where did those voices originate? How old was I? (Early days of school, when my parents divorced, when I was seven, puberty, and so on.)

Somatic Journaling

To begin, find a quiet place where you can be sure you will not be interrupted. When you sit down to write and reflect, you might begin with reflections on your day, celebrations as well as places where you felt challenged. "I felt so upset at lunch when....""I was filled with joy watching my son/daughter..."

Identify the stimulus that triggered the sensation. "I got a call from..."

Identify what you were feeling and where it showed up in your body. (My belly tensed. My throat was tight. My head hurt. I couldn't breathe.)

If you have space and time, reflect on what stories may be attached to the feelings and sensations and to the needs that were trying to be met—the deeper motivations. For example: "I felt angry when_____happened, and I noticed my belly was tense/upset/nauseas, which made me remember/think about...."

Here are some somatic questions to ask yourself so you can explore any somatic visceral responses that come up for you as you write your somatic autobiography and daily journaling:

- Where did I learn that?

- How do I organize around it?

- How does it feel? Where do I feel alive?

- Where do I feel deadened?

- How is that life/deadness being expressed?

- What does the feeling tell me?

- How do I interpret it?

- What kind of pain/pleasure was it?

- Did it feel muscular, skeletal?

- How is it, exploring those feelings? Where is the exploration leading?

- Where is that living in me?

- What do I notice?

- What does that open for me?

- How am I doing?

- Any images or thoughts provoked?

- What is my predominant emotion?

- Where did I learn that?

- What is its trajectory? What is it connected to? Moving away from?

We can only experience pain when it touches beauty.

Marshall Rosenberg

CHAPTER SIX

Two Sides of Gratitude

Celebration and Mourning

I once led a weekend training called "Embodying NVC" at a local YMCA for a group of 20 adults ranging in age from 20 to 75. After we explored some self-empathy skills with the Spiral Blend Practice (page 145), I spoke about the healing that comes through "mourning" and "celebration" in times of change. I re-framed both as expressions of gratitude. Celebration is the sweet feeling you have when someone or something that you love meets your deep needs and is present in your life. Mourning is the sadness or grief you feel when you miss something or someone that you love.

As we resumed the practice, I noticed Diana, a 30ish woman, sitting next to me, quietly weeping. When I asked what was going on for her, she said: "I was feeling sad about a dear friend of mine who recently died, and when you re-framed grief as gratitude, I felt my sadness as love and appreciation for my friend. Until now, I did not know what to do with the pain I felt deep in my chest. My tears are no longer something I need to hide away. Instead, they come to honor my friend who is no longer with me." Her tears continued in bittersweet release.

I asked her how the pain in her chest felt now, and she said that it had subsided somewhat—that it no longer hurt so much. She wept for a while, and then with a gentle smile said, "I feel good." She thanked the group and said: "I will leave to go home because I want to let the tears continue to come. It feels deeply healing, and it feels clear that this is all I need to do for now."

The celebration of mourning, when allowed to flow, is a sweet sadness that is healing. Becoming reacquainted with and listening empathically to the hurt places within us leaves us with a sweet melancholy, a feeling of grieving what we miss coupled with the joy of reuniting with what we love. This process brings a greater tolerance for and understanding of our emotions and more compassion for the emotional difficulties of others.

Crying and Dignity

Diana also shared something I hear often in trainings—that she felt a little embarrassed to cry in front of the others in the room. Respectfully, I asked whether she would be okay trying something with me, and she said yes. I asked her to look around the circle of participants. She noticed 16 sets of caring eyes. I asked the group, "If you feel more connected with Diana, and experience her tears as a gift in this moment, please raise your hands." Everyone raised hands. Then I asked, "Who felt themselves wanting to move away as Diana expressed her emotion?" No hands were raised.

This gave Diana a chance to check her internal stories about crying against the visible feedback from the people around her. I asked Diana how that feedback was for her to experience. Thoughtfully, she reflected that it was a bit "altering" in a good way. When I encounter those who feel the urge to move away from someone who is crying, I find that when we take it a little deeper, we usually encounter a story that equates crying with being weak or a burden for others. Following those stories to their source leads to insights and healing as well.

Almost always a participant's tears free emotions all around the room. In fact, in some cultures around the world, those who can cry readily are hired for weddings, funerals, and special occasions as "tear-looseners" because they are seen as being close to spirit, and their tears bring everyone closer to spirit for the occasion. Crying opens us to our interior and is a healthy release, as natural as burping and farting. As we drop the self-judgments about crying, we may even notice that crying feels good. My practice these days when tears come is to appreciate them as healing. Instead of hiding my face in my hands, I tend to sit up, explore how I feel, and look at who I am with, openly and with dignity. Sometimes I even catch myself smiling through the experience.

Loving Life

Our lives are in a constant state of change. Change often involves loss to be mourned as well as something new to be celebrated. The two sides of gratitude, simply put, are both a love of life. Embracing both is not only healthy but the better we can express our gratitude, the less prone we are to resentment, depression, despair, and violence. A deep, honest, authentic, expression of gratitude for something or someone you love is an agent of change and a gift to community.

A Mourning/Celebration Exercise

Think of someone you have loved who has died or is no longer in your life and allow the sadness of that loss to arise. Remember a time when that person was present, loving, and engaged with you. Identify and acknowledge your needs for love and support that were met at that time. Allow yourself to just feel the gratitude that arises. Breathing into it, let the gratitude become stronger to fill your emotional batteries. If a sweet melancholy arises, let it. It is healing. This is celebration and mourning. The are two sides of the same coin.

Gratitude is the first and mother of all practices. As infants, we are beings purely in need of help. We're fed, clothed, protected, soothed, and nurtured without offering much other than our being in return. All of us who have grown past childhood share this in common. Gratitude is the truth of our existence. Hanging out in gratitude is not telling life the way we want things to go in order for us to be happy; it's the practice of going with the moment and appreciating the truth of "I am where I am supposed to be." Self-pity and gratitude are choices. You can practice either one. Living in gratitude makes life not ordinary.

Life comes in waves. If you ask anyone who surfs what's required to ride a wave, they will tell you that you need to be present, balanced, have good timing, and trust that your practice and body will kick in. Imagine any challenging relationship, performance, or business situation—any of life's conflicts—as energy. Can you experience that conflict as an oncoming wave that offers an opportunity to surf, and the bigger the wave, the greater the sense of thrill and challenge? How you engage that wave of energy directly creates the outcome.

Imagine using some of the strategies we normally use in relationships to surf the wave:

Fool it.
Stand up to it and try to control it.
Be nice to it. Argue with it.
Dominate it.
Submit to it.
Try to manipulate it.

Instead: Accept it. Be curious. Be grateful.

S.U.R.F.I.N.G. CENTERING PRACTICE

You can't stop the waves, but you can learn to surf!

In this practice, we move through different centers in our bodies, being curious and with gratitude. Notice any places where you feel emotional or physical discomfort. By learning to tolerate your own feelings with love and patience, you increase your capacity for graciousness and dignity with others. The way to surf a wave is to be present and engaged and grateful for the opportunity to surf the wave. If you can relax, center, and balance so your body feels the wave's power, shifts, and movement, you can move and blend with it more effectively. This can be thrilling. Whether it is a wave or an insult thrown at you, by facing an experience in a relaxed, centered, balanced, and intuitive way, you can engage it synergistically, which will move you faster and farther than you might ever go alone.

Start as a sitting practice. The main attitude here is gratitude. Hold your head above your heart above your belly, paying attention to your vertical line. Soften your gaze or close your eyes. Let your tongue rest on the floor of your mouth. Lengthen the back of the neck, and imagine any emotional weight you are carrying falling off your shoulders for now. If this is perturbing, keep in mind that you can pick it back up when you finish. Unclench your sphincter muscles to feel your tail bone connect to the earth. Take in a deep and relaxing breath, and let out an audible "Ahhhhh" as you breathe out. Do this again. Begin a gentle, even breathing rhythm—up your back and down your front—and continue this circular breathing throughout the practice.

S: Shape

Put your attention into the area around the base of your tailbone. Imagine roots spiraling down into the earth, spreading out and connecting you to the ground, the dirt, the rocks, other roots, and organisms. Now follow your imagination above the ground to the plants, animals, all living creatures, water, the air, birds, sun, the sky, the stars, and all creation. Take this moment to honor and be grateful in your own way for the earth and nature that support you. Such gratitude connects us to all these resources.

U: Unify

Take a deep breath in, and as you feel the air fill your lungs, notice how good it feels! Expel the breath—all of it—and notice how good that also feels. Breathe up your back and down your front. Put your attention into the center of your belly. Just a couple of inches below the navel is an area referred to in Aikido as the *hara*. Aikido's physical movements emanate from the hara, which can be understood as the center of our spiritual confidence. Bring your attention to the space that is behind your belly, at your back. Feel into what supports you from behind and all that came before you. You can be selective. Invite the ancestors and older relatives who were healthy and whole (leave the crazy ones out), the teachers in your life, the great teachers on this planet past and present, all the wisdom contained in your genetic cellular history back to the beginning of life. You can imagine many hands holding you from behind. All this is behind you. Feel the support at your back. Bring in one at a time or a whole posse. Remember, you are not alone. There is always much to support you, no matter what you may think. Explore and do what feels best.

Let a sense of gratitude wash over you for all that supports you from behind. Now place your attention to your sides and imagine all those who walk beside you in your life—your friends, brothers and sisters, partners, and associates. Again, be as selective as you like.

Take a moment to be grateful for them.

Now place your attention in front of you, and imagine all the young ones who remind you to play, be curious, walk in wonder and awe, who will go beyond you to connect you to the future, and who make it all worthwhile. Take a moment, and in your own way, be grateful for the young ones.

*At your own time and speed, as a daily practice, you can place your attention on those people on any side of you who are/were less easy for you to be with. Take time to look beneath their words and strategies to our common humanity. Appreciate how these difficult people are potentially your best training partners. I re-frame these people as my "Lucifers." Lucifer means "Light Bringer." These people shine a light in places inside you that I might never find without them. In time, with practice, you can build your capacity for loving and valuing those who challenge you in your life.

R: Resource

Breathe up your back and down your front. Now bring your attention to the center of your solar plexus, around the hollow of your chest, below the heart region and above the belly. Take a moment to appreciate and give gratitude for who you are and all that you bring to the world. Many of us have never taken time to make an inventory of these resources and fully appreciate them.

If this feels lovely, stay with it and sit with that. If you notice somewhere inside yourself sensations of uneasiness, sadness, pain, contraction, emptiness, or the like, bring your attention to where that feeling is in your body. Ask yourself the following question, and listen closely to the very first intuitive answer that comes into your thoughts: "How old was I when I learned this?"

If you do not get an answer, try again until you do. Any answer is useful. Answers could be at birth, 2, 4, 6, 10, 32, or 50, even before birth. Whatever age you initially say, take note. If it was when you were an infant or newborn, imagine holding yourself at that young age, and take a moment to be grateful for the beautiful child within you. If you were a young child, let her nudge her way into your lap. Invite this child with love and gratitude. Invite the pimply faced teen to come sit beside you. Take some time with the age that stands out, one at a time. In each sitting, imagine holding, listening, walking with, or tending to these different ages of yourself in ways you would have loved. Be patient with each younger "self." He or she may hurt and feel unseen. Take this moment to be grateful for each of these ages of yourself. *Take a moment to be grateful for your present self.* If this is a regular practice, it may be most useful to spend time with only one or two of these ages of yourself a day. Keep in mind that this is not about wallowing in the past; it is more of a catch and release. Catch those early moments, notice them, appreciate the deeper needs, then let them go.

F: Field

Breathe up your back and down your front. Connecting and breathing, bring your attention from the earth, through all your relations, to your self. Now bring your attention to your heart, pulsating, radiating in all directions, offering and receiving, connecting to all other hearts, to all life, giving meaning through all you feel. *In this moment, in your own way, find gratitude for your beautiful, connective heart. Honor it.*

I: Inspire

Breathe up your back and down your front. Breathe up through the earth you sit on, through all your relations, your self, the heart. Now move up to your throat region. When you are rooted in the nature that supports you, all your relations, yourself and your heart, you can know what is true for you and rest in this knowing as you express yourself with confidence. *Take a moment to be grateful for your ability to speak and honor your truth.*

N: Navigate

Breathe up your back and down your front. Breathe up from the earth, all your relations, your self, heart, voice, and now up to your forehead, just between and above your eyes. When you are connected with all these resources and relations that are always available, you can trust that you know what is true for you and navigate from that place with confidence. *Take a moment to be grateful for that.*

G: Generate

Breathe up your back and down your front. Breathe up from the earth and through all your relations, your self, your heart, your voice, up to your forehead, and now to the crown of your head. As you breathe, imagine extending a vertical line down to the center of the earth and then back up through the centers of your body, through the crown of your head, and to the sky. Fully connecting to all our resources in ourselves prepares us to generate the future we aspire to. *In your own way, be grateful for the present moment.*

A Journaling Practice

Controlled experiments have shown that people who record things they're grateful for experience an increase in joy, happiness, and overall satisfaction with their lives. When you focus on things you're grateful for, you amplify good memories about the past. The University of Southern California did a 10-week study with three groups: Group 1 wrote five things a day they were grateful for with general comments. Group 2 got specific and wrote five sentences on one thing they were grateful for. Group 3 wrote ways they were better off and more grateful than others. The people in Group 2 were generally more elated, excited, alert, less sad, and less lethargic. The test result: details = dividends. For 10 weeks, keep a journal, and each day choose one person or thing you are grateful for. Write five things about it that you love.

Learning Through the Body

Uncrimping a water hose allows more water to flow through it. Similarly, when we center ourselves, our bodies relax so more energy can flow through us and the more energy that flows, the more excitement and joy we can feel. Attending to what we are feeling brings us into the present. Opening to, rather than squeezing off, some parts of our lived experience results in a stronger presence that is felt by others. Learning through the body returns us again and again to the energy that presently wants to be lived—listening for and hearing the subtle urge for a new job or lifestyle, to release a long-held resentment, or perhaps an unacknowledged desire to show more gratitude to a friend.

(It is important to note that—as valuable as it is to reconcile our inner splits— there are times when some individuals compartmentalize the pain of deep trauma as a protective mechanism because the awareness of the trauma would be too much for their system to handle. These are the rare splits that are so incompatible with one's well-being that they must be stored away deep in the unconscious.)

This day and present moment is a "present" unlike any other moment. Gratitude for the life that is given to us is at the heart of gracious living. A wide-eyed child or the elder entering her last days looks at a starlit sky and watches the clouds go by with awe. Look at the sky. When was the last time you just looked at the sky? Every cloud is so different. Look into the eyes of each person you meet. Each face has a unique, astonishing story of different places, ancestors, and experiences connected to a unique past. Each of us is a mystery that can never fully be known. When we encounter another person and are truly present to the experience, it is transformative—like drinking from a deep, pure well. So much of what we call mundane is so easy to take for granted. Open the fridge and grab a snack, call   a friend on the phone, fill a glass with clean water, switch the light on to read a book. There are so many people who only dream of such miraculous gifts. If you open your heart and let gratitude for all these blessings flow through you, everyone you meet will be blessed by your presence.

Here is an old Kabbalistic wisdom story I first heard told by Rabbi David Cooper that offers insights to gratitude and graciousness. Graciousness welcomes you at the door and lets you know when it is time to leave. It is an intuitive "felt quality" that is experienced by others as genuine in a way that honors all—and   is possessed by true leaders.

The Copper Kopeck

In the 18th century, there lived a couple in St. Petersburg who were about to be married. Just before the wedding, the bridegroom was kidnapped and held for ransom—10,000 rubles—an extremely large sum of money at the time, and especially for this couple, who were quite poor. In those days, such kidnappings were not uncommon. The police and military frequently took into custody or kidnapped Jews and held them for ransom.

Jewish law directed that the community do anything needed in order to save a Jewish life, even if it meant selling their most sacred scrolls. The family of the bridegroom approached the elders of the community—three Rabbis who became well known in time—Rabbis Zalman, Yitzhak, and Mendel. For such a large sum of money, not much could be done. The only person with that kind of money was Ze'ev, but they argued that he was such a miser that he would never help. He never contributed money to anything—ever.

Rabbi Zalman believed he could be successful talking to Ze'ev. The other two thought he was crazy and tried to dissuade him, but he would have none of that. He said he was going and began to leave when the other two Rabbis said they would accompany him because Ze'ev lived on the rough side of town. Rabbi Zal- man agreed on the condition that the other two would not interfere and would remain quiet.

When they arrived, Ze'ev met them at the door, surprised but honored to find these three distinguished men at his home. A little suspicious, he welcomed them in and offered tea. After some pleasantries, Rabbi Zalman began to tell the sad story of the abduction of the young man, who was an orphan with no real family, a hard life, and who, just one week before the wedding, had been taken by the police on fake charges and would not be freed unless they were given the 10,000 ruble ransom.

As Rabbi Zalman told the story, the other rabbis silently watched tears well up in Ze'ev's eyes. When he finished, Ze'ev said: "Such a travesty. I am deeply moved to help." He reached deep into his pockets, into regions that had not seen the light of day for many years, and pulled out one very old, dirty, rusty kopek. He handed this tiny sum to Rabbi Zalman, who exclaimed: "Thank you so much. Blessings on you and your family and all you do. May God shine his light on your business and health. Thank you." He went on and on, praising with abundant gratitude.

The two other rabbis, who promised to keep their mouths shut, watched in disbelief the high praise over such a paltry contribution.

As the three rabbis prepared to leave, Ze'ev asked them to wait. He said, "You have touched me so much with this story, I feel that I must give you more." He reached deep into his other pocket, into another place untouched for a very long time, and pulled out one more very small, rusty, old copper kopeck. A new round of praises and blessings that lasted another 10 minutes followed this. Finally, out on the street, walking away from the house. Rabbi Yitzhak said: "What a waste of time! We just spent an hour for two lousy kopeks!"

"Hush," whispered Rabbi Zalman.

When they were about a hundred feet from the house, the front door opened and Ze'ev called out, "Rabbis, come back."

Ze'ev was waving a 5-ruble note. Rabbi Zalman received this with much appreciation. A few minutes later, Ze'ev donated 50 rubles, and soon after, another five hundred, and then one thousand. Finally, he wrote out a check for the full amount of 10,000 rubles.

Walking away, the two rabbis were stunned and asked, "What just happened?" and "How did you know he would give so much?"

Rabbi Zalman replied: "Our hearts' walls can shield our hearts, which keeps things from getting in, but also from getting out. There is no way to remove the heart's protection all at once. First you must find the tiniest crack, and then each small opening of generosity and gratitude makes way for another. The notion of slowly dismantling such barriers is the key to all success, to deep learning, for work, for relationships, for love, as well as charity. Each good deed builds a capacity to do more. The greatest accomplishments often begin with something very small, like a copper kopeck. Let yourself learn slowly, widening the crack until at some point you will be able to pass through the opening easily."

The story of the dirty penny is a metaphor for attaining greater awareness. In order to do so we must find a way to make a crack in our own barriers so the light of awareness can shine through. The story suggests that we open to ourselves one step at a time. Eventually this crack in the dam reveals a great reservoir available to us, once we remove our finger from the crack in the dam of self-identity. If we have the qualities to do so, we will be flooded in light. I refer to the same qualities of presence that allow you to "get out of your own way" in order for empathy to occur.

To develop the muscles for gratitude, start small, and as with any learning process, build it slowly. Breathe in, and just appreciate the air passing through your lungs and how good it feels, then breathe out, too.

Appreciation of life as a regular practice can change everything: the people we meet, the work we do, as well as bringing more joy to our intimate relationships. Starting today, how would it be to begin a new relationship in which you give gratitude for everything your body does for you? Forgetting to appreciate this and instead judging and even feeling ashamed of our bodies is a form of self-abuse. Regardless, our bodies love us unconditionally. Every time you eat, bathe, walk, sing, love another, or sleep can be a moment of gratitude. This practice would surely change everything and be a powerful building block for all relationships.

> Revisit the S.U.R.F. practice(page 12) and try "gratitude" as the resource. Ask yourself how it would feel to have a little more gratitude? Feel how and where in your body you feel blocked from gratitude. Write down the thing that you are most frightened to be grateful for. Ask yourself what scares you most about this? Look at it. If you can do that and have the courage to write it down, it will be like a contract that says, "You will learn to appreciate this," and that is freeing!

If you feel blocked from feeling gratitude, try this:

"Forgive yourself"

Peter, a dear friend who struggled with cancer for quite a while, died last year—for a moment. And then he was resuscitated. The second he came back, he opened his eyes, looked at his daughter, and said, "Forgive yourself." In that life-and-death moment of clarity, I believe Peter was referring to the deeper nature of forgiveness, not the familiar, often somewhat superior "I forgive you" that comes out of "you should" or "I deserve," like the punishing God, where we sit in judgment of each other and lack understanding. This old, familiar concept of forgiveness is what is experienced when emotions and bitterness are not healed but have settled enough to exact an apology and subsequently reach some complicit agreement that the "forgiven" injury shall not be repeated. There is an element of punishment inherent in this type of forgiveness.

A deeper, more realized experience of forgiveness brings with it a change of heart and spirit—after which every seeming injury, injustice, or rejection—whether past, present, or future becomes an essential note in the music of living, however discordant it may sound to our superficial hearing. This experience excludes nothing. Marshall Rosenberg said, "All violence is the result of people tricking themselves into believing that their pain derives from other people and that consequently those people deserve to be punished." "Every criticism, judgment, diagnosis, and **expression** of anger is the **tragic expression of an unmet need**." What this implies is that in the moment of true forgiveness, all one's "short comings" and "weaknesses", all of the tragic ways that we can express our unmet needs, are included, being at the same time both remembered and known as the essential darkness that has revealed to us the light. Forgiveness must look at the darkness—our shadows—and the weakness, and remember it. True forgiveness experiences the darkness with joy, as essential to wholeness and where our humanity is revealed. Forgiveness in its wholeness requires humility and taking full responsibility for one's own thoughts, perceptions, feelings, and judgments of self and other.

This time sit with the S.U.R.F. Practice and the quality of forgiveness. Ask yourself, "How would it feel if I felt a little more forgiveness". Let the quality arise without attaching it to forgiving anyone specific, even yourself. Just the quality. Be open and curious to what your intuitive body shows you.

Gratitude Encourages Forgiveness

There will always be times when something we do or say turns out to be less than helpful, and even worse, damaging to ourselves or others. We cannot always be in tune with our feelings and needs, fully centered, and in touch with our empathy and desire to hold everyone's needs with compassion. Forgiveness is a personal decision to move on and let go of the feeling of being wronged and/or being wrong, to not be ruled by it, have it influence our actions, or how we look at the world. Much of the power of gratitude is because of the co-occurrence of forgiveness. Gratitude and forgiveness are distinct attributes but share a common quality of empathy.

Forgiveness presents an opportunity to recognize what happened, take stock, determine what's truly important, and remember who we want to be. It doesn't mean we forget or accept the action as good; it means we discern and move forward in a healthier, more-enlightened, more-loving manner. Learning from the past is essential; living in the past is deadening. We can't change our own or anyone's past. The path of gratitude and forgiveness is in the present moment. Choosing forgiveness is an act of self-love. It removes the suffering from memories of incidents that we regret or wish we had handled differently—more in harmony with what's really important to us. Accepting forgiveness in order to understand the mistakes we have made and to gain the wisdom to not make the same mistakes again helps us to heal and transform. Through love and forgiveness, we can grow our capacity to share love without fear and find communion and reunion. The benefits go on and on. People who practice gratitude and forgiveness are likely to have lower rates of heart disease, fewer stress-related health issues, a greater sense of self-worth, closer relationships, less anger, fewer feelings of loneliness, fewer depressive symptoms, greater acceptance, and more empathy and self-compassion.

Thanks in Advance

To think, speak, and do something you think is impossible is not possible. Creation must include a gut knowing ahead of time. This is an act of faith. It is gratitude in advance before and for creation, which is a key to creation. It is what the master of any art does. Mastery knows in advance that the deed is done, celebrates that, blesses it, and if there is some aspect of the creation that is not satisfying, changes it.

Wherever you go, preach the gospel, and if necessary, use words.

St Francis of Assisi

CHAPTER SEVEN

The Signals We Give

We Feel Before We Think

L iving in relationship is so challenging, in part, because everyone is always transmitting the qualities of their emotional states. How we comport ourselves communicates volumes and is often more impactful than our words. No matter how much we may try to hide it, our bodies are incapable of lying. Sometimes we feel centered and happy; other times we feel tense and contracted. We can know whether another person is open to us or not by how our own body responds to theirs. Beneath the words and stories we tell, every encounter is an interplay of nonverbal forces. Our unique virtues, neuroses, traits, patterns, and behaviors collide, play, compete, irritate, haunt, hook, draw, excite, seduce, and enhance one another. Some people fill us with joy, while others seem to suck all the air out of our chests. Consciously and unconsciously, we leak and leach, share our overflows, and fill each other's gaps. The presence of another—a friend, a family member, a stranger, a Mother Theresa or a Hitler–can impact and alter our whole way of being.

As we explore nonverbal communication, let's remain aware of the power of words. Words can free our thinking or imprison our souls. The words we say are only the tip of the iceberg compared to the messages we project through body language, voice tone, gestures, facial expression, and other nonverbal cues. At the same time, our language patterns reinforce cultural imperatives, which may or may not be helpful. Used over and over, speech patterns become deeply embedded and are challenging to change because they exist beneath our radar in daily interactions and are integrally connected to what we communicate non-verbally. We've all experienced times when our words, although carefully chosen with good intentions, leave the listener(s) feeling upset and confused. Others can sense when our words and feelings do not align. It breeds mistrust.

Who Are We Fooling?

Here is an exercise I share in my trainings that demonstrates how difficult, if not impossible, it is to clearly express one thing while feeling another.

> First, think of something that makes you genuinely smile. Keeping that smile, speak about something that truly disgusts you. Any semblance of that original smile will invariably begin to feel and look fake. Conversely, try to maintain a grimace while speaking about something that is truly joyful. Invariably, a smile peeks through. So, it is worthwhile to keep in mind that on some level, when we try to hide our feelings, we are not fooling anyone.

All spiritual and mystical traditions emphasize contemplative silence and rec-ognize that words cannot fully describe the true nature of reality. Words can be poetic, understanding, and kind, but words alone neither love nor sustain us and, in fact, at times can become a barrier to our interconnectedness. Words are only signposts pointing to the things they describe. Learning to follow our senses releases us from the limits of our words to hear the quiet regions of our intuition.

The Sixth Sense

Sensitivity to the needs of others requires the development of not only the five senses we are familiar with, but the sixth sense as well. The "sixth sense" is our intuitive ability to perceive the elusive signals that are beyond the range of our physical senses, to discern whether someone is a friend or a foe, and to sense what lies behind the masks people wear. In Aikido training, we learn to listen with our whole body, to bring all our senses to bear as one unified synesthetic organ of perception. This helps us sense actions forming in the body of another before any threatening move is made, before any physical or verbal action is initiated.

All around us there is evidence of the ability to receive perceptions and impres-sions in ways beyond hearing, tasting, touching, smelling, and seeing. Animals demonstrate this all the time. They sense immediately when we are afraid. Plants thrive better with those who care about them more than with those who care less. We all have this perceptive ability and can hone it with practice.

Although this is not a scientific document, what follows are some of the new discoveries in neural science regarding the body's intelligence and its role in how we perceive and relate to the world. Scientists in the field disagree, yet there is ample phenomenological evidence collected over many decades of study and testing that point in the directions suggested.

The Heart-Brain Matrix

Our language offers insights into the qualities of the heart—big-hearted, heart-felt, heart's desire, kind-hearted, courage of heart, sweetheart. When we do not feel connected with the heart's messages, we may use the words heartsick, heart-broken, downhearted, heartache, and heartless.

When I first met Marshall Rosenberg and began practicing NVC, I tried to emulate his skill and ability to empathize. The image this evoked for me was to somehow beat back the brambles and thickets that had grown over the path from my brain to my heart. The task felt daunting. Appreciating some of the recent discoveries in science helped along the way.

Consider that 60 to 65 percent of your heart's cells are actually neural cells, the same kind of cells that make up your brain. The heart possesses its own nervous system and is inextricably linked as a specialized part of the brain. The heart processes meaning within a variety of emotional experiences and has its own stored memories. There are many stories of people who have had heart transplants that have suddenly been overwhelmed with the thoughts, memories, dreams, tastes, and desires of the organ's donor.

Approximately two gallons of blood move through 60,000 miles of blood vessels in each of our bodies. If you took all the arteries, veins, and capillaries in one adult body and arranged them end-to-end, they'd encircle the earth twice! We generally think of the heart as a pump that moves blood throughout our bodies. The force from the heart is powerful. It has enough force to shoot water six feet into the air. But in order to pump your blood through the entire length of your body's circulatory system, the actual amount of force that would be needed could push a 100-pound weight one mile high. Contrary to popular belief, the heart does not pump blood through the whole body. The whole body, including the blood, pumps and moves our blood through our whole body, in unison.

How is this possible?

Our hearts are vastly more than a muscular pump. The heart is, in fact, a highly sensitive organ of perception, a powerful electromagnetic generator and receiver. Blood is an electrical conductor—there are magnetic particles within it. The heart generates an electromagnetic energy field that emits and receives varied and complex signals.

Modern medicine has produced mechanical pacemakers that people use to stimulate their hearts to beat. Nature's original pacemakers in our bodies are large groupings of cells—millions of them—that emit rhythmic beats, oscillating like synchronized swimmers or tuning forks, in resonance with one another. As new cells grow, they join and entrain. Millions and millions of cells, beating in unison, send out increasingly powerful electromagnetic waves as they synchronize.

The organized patterns of energy your heart sends out have been shown to directly affect the functioning of other organs and organisms outside your heart. The cells and organs of our bodies live interdependently and are in constant, dynamic communication within the greater ecosystem. One needs only to take a walk through a wild landscape or view an ocean vista to get a better sense of this interconnectedness.

Our hearts, like radar towers, continually scan for communications and information. When the electromagnetic field from one heart encounters another's, we emphatically experience a range of emotional impressions. When it receives impulses from other electromagnetic fields, the heart experiences alterations in its own electromagnetic spectrum. The way the field is altered conveys information, much like a radio receiver picks up various stations. When our individual fields of energy patterns meet and perturb one another, we experience this as emotions. When two or more fields synchronize, information is conveyed. Like notes played on a piano, these encounters can create beautiful harmonies, dissonance that is disturbing, or various other intriguing or diverse combinations.

The heart is extremely sensitive, and the slightest emotional change—due either to internal or external factors—quickly manifests itself as a change in the heart rate and the electromagnetic field it generates. The resonance of our hearts with other electromagnetic fields is something we are all familiar with, whether we are conscious of it or not. The womb is our first matrix of life. It provides us with safety and nourishment as well as many basic needs, such as the loving touch of empathy.

In a sense, empathy is our first language. It's how mother and child initially communicate. A mother's developed heart communicates to the infant's heart what it needs for its own development in the critical first months after birth as well. We grow in our mother's electromagnetic fields in-utero. We are born into our mother's empathic field and within the greater electromagnetic field of the earth. This relationship and information exchange is deep within our cellular memories.

Let the Heart Lead

"On your journey, throw your heart out in front of you, and then follow it," was the advice of a Suquamish tribal elder when a group of people, including my son, set off to walk across the US in remembrance of Hiroshima. We've been habituated through our schooling and Western culture to locate the center of our intelligence in our brain, not our heart. Most likely, if you ask someone who was raised in an intact indigenous culture where their center of wisdom resides, they will point to their heart, because that is what their culture practices.

World-famous boxer Joe Frazier said, "When you lead from your head, you get pounded." When you are "in your head," you are taking information from past and present experiences, evaluating, and choosing strategies. This works for the most part and is often an effective strategy, especially for a fast thinker. Still, there is a qualitative difference that exists in the connection you have with someone when the heart is involved.

The Heart Does Not Judge

Our thinking processes, such as when we are doing math, scheduling our days, or making judgments, are linear. Linear thinking sends out signals that do not invite entrainment from the rest of the body. Entrainment is the harmonious cooperation and order we feel in relationship to what is all around us. We entrain to the rhythms around us all the time, although often we are unaware of it. An example is that young women who are roommates often menstruate at the same time.

When the head is judging, the heart does not entrain with it. When we judge others, coherence happens less. Another way of understanding this is that the heart does not judge. If you are busy judging someone and think you are being heartfelt, think again. You probably are not. Coherence is a state of optimal clarity, perception, and performance. Coherence refers to the synchronization of our physical, mental, and emotional systems (internal consensus). It can be measured by our heart-rhythm patterns. The more balanced and smooth they are, the more in sync, or coherent, we are.

Heart-centered processes initiate coherence, in which the rhythm of the heart sets the rhythm for your entire system. The heart's rhythmic beat influences the brain's functions that control the nervous system, cognitive functioning, and hormones. Coherence enhances intuitive awareness and improves decision-making capabilities that go beyond the normal capacity of thinking alone. Global coherence refers to the mental, physical, emotional, and spiritual well-being of the greater humanity acting in concert with their own hearts, each other, and nation-to-nation in harmony with the living earth.

Heart-focused perception does not habituate, so perception through the heart remains new through each experience. There is no single conversation with the heart, no grand fit that declares you are now enlightened and can relax. It is not about memorization. It is simply the practice of being open to what the heart says in this moment. In other words, you are present when the heart leads, and the good news is that this is something you can consciously practice. Think of the consequences, especially in long-term relationships: *every moment that you lead from your heart is experienced as new.*

Calming and Settling

Centering your attention in the heart can shift automatic, reactive, flight/fight responses. At the instant of a stressful, triggering moment, *with the enlistment of the creative forebrain*, you can shift your focus away from the perceived impending disaster and direct it to the heart or some pleasant visual image and, in doing so, sidestep a myriad of justifications for offense, revenge, or anger. This creative act enables you to turn your back on millions of years of genetically encoded survival reflexes in favor of the intelligence of compassion. Remembering a moment of love or joy directs a high frequency signal from the prefrontal cortex to the limbic heart. The heart automatically answers on the same frequency, lifting us into a higher level of creative dynamic that defuses reactions and opens us to resources unavailable through either intellect or imagination alone.

Many studies have shown what happens when the heart's electromagnetic field is intentionally changed as a person shifts his or her attention. When you move away from judging thoughts or questions such as "What will I do today?" and shift your focus to your heart, to your breath, or to calming external stimuli such as a stream or a plant, the heartbeat slows and begins a transformational cascade that alters your physiological, emotional, and cognitive processes. The sympathetic nervous system connects us with our fight/flight reactions; the parasympathetic nervous system shifts us to rest and ease. Placing your attention on external stimuli or your heart brings both of these systems online in a balanced manner. The more meaning, care, gratitude, and interest in the quality of your attention, the greater the beneficial physiological changes that occur. You can recognize this state physically as more softly focused eyes, a slowing of the heart- beat, and the body relaxing.

Quieting

Sit or stand in an upright, comfortable way and put your attention on something around you that is pleasant to view. Look out the window to see the moonlight or a flower or simply light a candle. Allow yourself to look at whatever you've chosen, noticing its colors, shape, and textures. Notice how it feels to you. Notice how you feel. Right at that moment, your body's physiological functions will shift in a very noticeable manner. Keep your attention there instead of on expectations of what you think you should be feeling. Otherwise, this exercise in focus will not work. Try the exercise again, only this time, focus your attention down into your heart. See whether you can breathe quietly and feel your heart beating in your chest and just appreciate that it is doing so. Keep your attention there, and notice how this feels. Notice any internal shifts that take place as you do so.

Centers of Intelligence

Within our bodies, we have other biological oscillators besides the heart, which weave and dance together to manage our systems. Recent neuro-cardiological studies suggest how the heart, with its extensive intrinsic nervous system processes, learns, and stores information and makes functional decisions. Parallel discoveries in the newer field of neuro-gastroenterology have identified another "brain" in the enteric nervous system—our gut. Like the heart, our gastrointestinal (GI) tract is lined with neural cells and has its own extensive, elegant nervous system. Both the heart and the gut have unique functions that pick up and process critical information from inside and outside the body in many ways that are different from the thinking faculties of the brain in our head.

One of the first steps in learning Aikido is to become familiar with our "*hara*," the gut center, located a couple of inches below the belly button. It's considered a place of intuition and confidence. It is also the body's physical center of gravity and where all Aikido technique organizes and moves from. Just as a gyroscope provides a stable point of reference for navigating a ship, the hara provides a place of stability and balance for the body. Planets draw from their center as we draw from our center. Good balance and physical technique depends on that, too. In sports, such as skating or skiing in which you move at high speeds, a shift in the hara becomes immediately obvious.

The heart, the gut, and the brain are each powerful oscillators. In different situations, entrainment boosts the power of whichever of these oscillators becomes the main focus. When the gut center is activated, a sense of settled-ness arises that allows the other centers to work more fully. If the belly is disconnected, the heart must become tough instead of soft and feeling, while the head tries to be confident. When the brain entrains to the heart, the brain becomes more in tune and connected with the body. When the heart leads, the brain shifts to coherence, affecting the cortex, which works directly with perception and learning. The heart has no principle except love. When the heart is connected to the head and belly, it becomes soft and able to feel. When the heart is not connected to the belly, it needs to be tough and can overwork and become exhausted.

When the brain's oscillating wave patterns become the main pattern, over time the heart begins to lose coherence as it starts to relate to a linear waveform that is not dynamically responsive to the moment. It makes sense that in a culture where schools are oriented to favor the brain almost exclusively over the heart, reward thinking over feeling and hierarchy over empathy, that heart disease is the number one killer in the United States. Love, gratitude, and forgiveness are states of mind. Self-pity and the feeling of being victimized are light-years from a life lived in spirit and truth that is open to the heart.

Once open to the heart, we can recognize the universe as benevolent and the self to be the center of that benevolence. When our mind, heart, and belly entrain—that is, when their pulses synchronize with one another—this produces a harmonized state that can be quite powerfully moving. Our hearts, heads, and bellies entrained make for courageous, compassionate, intuitive, meaningful action and leadership. Heartfelt leadership internally organizes the body; externally, it moves others to collaborate as it promotes meaningful relationship. Joseph Chilton Pearce connects the dots: "Our body and brain form an intricate web of coherent frequencies organized to translate other frequencies and nestled within a nested hierarchy of universal frequencies."

The electromagnetic waves your heart emits are 5,000 times more powerful than your head. This electromagnetism is measurable up to 10 feet from the body. Although we can measure this electromagnetism with modern instruments, the depth and nature of the information encoded within it is far more than what we read on our instruments. Electromagnetic signals received and experienced as emotions by the heart have embedded meaning. Just as meaning can be drawn from the visual and audio signals that we receive, meaning is drawn from emotions through empathic listening that is felt. Over time and evolution, all living organisms have learned to use these fields as a medium to communicate. There is a constant mix and blending flow of information-loaded electromagnetic fields. It is part of the communication dynamic used to strengthen cooperative interactions of living organisms within ecosystems, an aspect of our co-evolutionary interdependence.

AN INNER CONSENSUS PROCESS

Consensus is the model our intentional community chose from the start. In time, we discovered it to be a way of life whose principles, similar to NVC, inform the practices while the practices slowly reveal insights regarding its principles. Both consensus and NVC offer guidance to navigate relationships with empathy, grace, and an appreciation of the messiness inherent to enduring relationships.

What Consensus and NVC are not:

- Not just a set pattern of rules or a process.
- Not about taking sides.
- Not about personal agendas.
- Not about compromising your needs.

What Consensus and NVC are:

- Valuing the process as much as the outcome.

- Developing emotional literacy.

- Ontological practices—a whole way of life.

- Building a capacity to stay open, transparent, responsible, and accountable in the midst of conflict and relationship.

- Holding a commitment to meeting everyone's needs, and not at the expense of one another.

- Reflect the uniqueness of each group.

- Developing the sense of "we are all in this together"

- Developing the capacity to move rapidly between group and self-awareness.

- *A healthy process is the goal, and the goal is the process.*

Empathic listening supports our integrity as organisms. Theologian, philosopher and physician Albert Schweitzer said, "Until he extends the circle of his compassion to all things, man will not himself find peace."

Here is a process that combines basic NVC skills of self-empathy and mediation to help resolve internal conflicts in order to build an inner consensus that honors the different voices inside and around you. The facilitator in this process is you. Mediating internal consensus builds the same skills and processes as a facilitator would use for mediating others. As with a circle of individuals, the facilitator's job is to maintain a sense of structure that allows every voice to be heard and acknowledged equally and fairly. Also, just as you would call a meeting to address a specific subject, when you call a meeting within yourself, always keep in mind why you are having it. Consensus meetings (especially with others) are more effective and more meaningful when they are called to address clear needs. Practicing this alone requires some imaginative muscle. Working the process will develop your abilities to explore your inner world at will. If you are working with a partner, have him or her sit beside you and follow this centering practice together:

Set Up

1. Find a comfortable spot, perhaps a quiet room or a nice place out in nature. Sit or stand, relaxed and vertical, with belly, heart, and head aligned. Imagine the soles of your feet if you are standing or your sit bone if you are seated, opening to the earth. Take several deep, relaxing breaths and let out an audible "ahhhhh" sound as you exhale. Now, focus on the qualities of intention you would like to bring to the conversation, such as respect, inclusiveness, and/or gratitude. You will use this intention to create an "empathy field" in which to hold all the voices that speak during the conversation. This step is similar to calling up a quality in the S.U.R.F. Practice, in which you ask the body a question and await the answer. Embellish this opening ritual in ways that fit you. Light a candle, ring a chime, drink some tea...

2. Now identify and articulate the internal conflict for which you called this meeting. Articulate what you want to address as clearly and concisely as you can. A good facilitator prepares for a meeting by articulating clearly what needs to be discussed and opening the conversation with clear, discerning questions. Usually there is some need and emotional pain that draws you into this process. Try to clearly identify where there is conflict so you can articulate a question that will form the basis of the conversation.

3. Welcome the participants as valuable and essential. Each organ of our body has intelligence. The more you acknowledge each, the more sense of aliveness there will be in the organ. Energy follows attention. Acknowledge the presence of your head, your heart, your gut, and your feet. Other voices may surprise you and want to be included, so welcome them as they arrive (your back, solar plexus, genitals, skin, etc.) They may be invited into the conversation at any time.

4. Set the ground rules: *One voice at a time. No cross talk.*

Sometimes I imagine a talking stick that is passed from one participant to another. Whoever has the stick talks without interruption until the stick is passed on— first the heart, then the gut, then back to the heart, and so on. As a facilitator, be strict about no cross talk. Skillfully learning to hold the space to hear one voice at a time requires some practice.

5. Begin with a question that is well considered.

Go to the participant with the most energy to speak, ask a question, and then await an answer. For example, say, "Heart, is it truly in our best interest to be alone tonight or to talk with my partner about the difficulties I am having with him at the moment? or, "Gut, is continuing at this job in my highest interest?"

Carefully listen to whichever voice you are working with. Ask a question and listen for a first and most immediate response. If one is not forthcoming, the facilitator can prompt with a suggestion like, "What is your first thought?" or "best guess?"

It is common for some voices to take a long time to check their answer. This act of self-censoring is often because other voices are chiming in, trying to influence the speaker in habitual ways. It can also be because that voice is not used to talking, much less being heard. For example, if you get the sense that the heart's answer is somehow tainted or odd, check in with it. In these confusing moments, where it is difficult to discern which voice is which, a skillful facilitator will slow things down and come back to the voice that had the floor or the talking stick last. You, as the facilitator, must check in with the heart by asking if the answer it spoke was its true answer, or if it is coming from somewhere else in the body. Often, the head will have chimed in because it is used to talking over the other voices. So, you can check in with the heart and ask if that was the heart's own voice, or if that was really the head speaking. The heart will check itself, and if that is the case, the facilitator can respectfully ask the head to wait its turn and assure it that it will have the time it needs to respond.

6. When the heart is done speaking, move to the next voice, such as the gut, and ask the same question or one that is now more appropriate. The gut will give its answer, and again, capturing the first thought is essential. The gut may also build on the conversation by offering its thoughts on what was previously contributed by the heart. Answers, for the most part, should be as short as possible, at the most 40words, preferably much less.

7. As each voice has a chance to speak, all of the others listen. In this example, the heart may want to forgive a friend's transgression; the head may want to talk it out immediately; the gut may be afraid of the unknown and hesitant; and the feet may say, "Stay." Each voice will offer its fears, reservations, excitement, desire, and the resources it can contribute.

8. With practice, the facilitator learns to hold the various contributions and direct the conversation forward in an orderly and sensitive manner. With the help of the facilitator's empathic listening, clear questions, and honest reflection, the deeper needs and unique resources of each contributor will become clearer and clearer.

9. In time, proposals for new actions, practices, choices, and other actions are offered and discussed collaboratively.

10. Any concerns are requested and brought up.

11. If there are concerns, the process continues.

12. Some participants' concerns may not call for actions; they just need to be voiced and let go of. Some concerns may require more conversations to resolve.

13. If there are no concerns that need attention, you have consensus.

With consensus comes commitment and implementation of new actions, choices, and practices. Moving from an integrated internal consensus, we transmit that unified state, and this, in turn, invites collaborative and harmonious interaction from others.

As we facilitate internally or with others, a core discipline in NVC is learning to discern between thoughts and feelings. Thoughts convey to the listener what we are thinking. Feelings convey to the listener our emotional and/or physical states. There are basically two types of feelings: emotional and physical.

Emotional: "I feel happy." (Feeling state)

Physical: "I feel cold." (Physical sensation state)

Generally, thoughts precede what we feel, and what we feel can dominate our thoughts. It is key in our internal mediation to know when the head is crowding the conversation with thoughts. Thoughts or beliefs (which are also thoughts) may be conscious or unconscious. Some of our core beliefs are buried deep below the surface of our awareness. A feeling can occur alone, and the mind will search for a thought—a story—to attach to it. That is precarious, because often the story actually isn't connected to the feeling, but our mind likes to have an explanation.

To be fully understood, especially when talking to our partners, spouses, children, and others, the listener needs to know the speaker's thoughts and feelings. It helps when feelings and thoughts are clearly differentiated for one simple reason: thoughts and feelings are two different types of data. More accurate data expressed gives us the best shot at being understood, appreciated, and cherished.

Something that clues us into when a thought is masquerading as a feeling is when we hear the word "I feel" followed by "like," "as if," or "that" and then a pronoun or a person's name. In these cases, the statement is usually a thought, not a feeling.

Let's explore this somatically:

1. Imagine you are speaking with someone. Now, with feeling, say each sentence below, one at a time, as if each were true for you. After each sentence, notice if what you are actually feeling is clear to you or not.

- I *feel* like you do not understand me.

- It *feels* as if we are never going to be together.

- I *feel* like you don't care about a clean house.

- I *feel* like Bob is heading for some big problems.

This first set of sentences each expresses a thought rather than a feeling. Receiving such statements will most likely be heard as an evaluation or criticism.

2. Now we'll add a true feeling after the word "feel." Read this set of sentences and see if what you feel is clearer:

- I *feel* frustrated when you tell me you will be on time and then you arrive late.

- I *feel* hopeless trying to find the connection I so want with you.

- I *feel* pissed when I come home to such a mess.

- I *feel* scared when I see Bob drinking every night.

The second set of sentences conveys clearly the feeling experienced by the speaker.

When our communication transmits that we are taking care to be responsible for our feelings, the listener will relax and is less likely to hear blame or receive what we say as a moral judgment. When expressing a feeling, take out the word "like," "that," or "as if" and fill in the blank with an actual feeling.

Be clear to make sure you are actually expressing what you feel, not an evaluation or veiled judgment.

SPEAKING FROM THREE CENTERS

This exercise is set up to help notice, locate, build a somatic impression, explore, and communicate through our mental, emotional, and intuitive centers of intelligence collectively and congruently.

Centering initiates effective action, emotional clarity, mental readiness, and spiritual vision. To move another's whole being you must engage your whole being. We are compassionate with ourselves when we are able to embrace all our parts and recognize the needs and values that each expresses.

Head: The head is the center of perception. When your head is connected to your belly and is freed up, this leads to intuitive knowing. When it is not connected, it overcompensates by trying to be strong. (The body is great at compensating.)

Heart: The heart is the center of feeling, compassion, and emotion. When we connect the heart with the other centers, it becomes soft and able to feel. When the heart is not supported by the belly—our gut sense—the heart gets tough, becomes overworked, and in time, exhausted.

Belly: The belly is the center of confidence, authenticity, and knowing. When we engage our gut sense, we have the experience of being centered, present, and settled. This allows the other centers to work more fully. In our culture, the belly—our intuition—generally is not emphasized in our education, so the heart becomes tough instead of soft and feeling, and the head tries to be smart and confident. We become headstrong and have a hard time with being open and inclusive.

The Practice

Choose a partner. One of you will receive a hard-to-hear request.

Part A

Your partner stands about eight feet away from you. Bring your attention to your head and thinking process. Your partner begins to walk toward you speaking a request such as, "I really need you to come to my home and help me get my house organized."

With attention to your head and thinking center say, "Stop!"

Ask your partner:

- How did that land on you?
- Did you feel like stopping?
- Was it powerful? Or not?
- Where do you feel it in your body?

Part B

Your partner stands about eight feet away from you. Bring your attention into your heart (emotional) center. Your partner begins to walk toward you speaking a request such as, "I really need you to come to my home and help me get my house organized."

Bring your attention into your heart center (touching it with your hand helps) and then say, "Stop!"

Ask your partner:

- How did that land on you?
- Did you feel like stopping?

- Was it powerful? Or not?
- Where do you feel it in your body?

Part C

Your partner stands about eight feet away from you. Bring your attention into your belly (intuitive) center. Your partner begins to walk toward you speaking a request such as, "I really need you to come to my home and help me get my house organized."

Bring your attention into your belly center, (touching it with your hand helps) and then say, "Stop!"

Ask your partner:

- How did that land on you?
- Did you feel like stopping?
- Was it powerful? Or not?
- Where do you feel it in your body?

Part D

Your partner stands about eight feet away from you. Bring your attention to your head, heart, and belly. Your partner begins to walk toward you speaking a request such as, "I really need you to come to my home and help me get my house organized."

Bring your attention into head, heart, and belly center together and then say, "Stop!"

Ask your partner:

- How did that land on you?
- Did you feel like stopping?
- Was it powerful? Or not?
- Where do you feel it in your body?

Part E

Your partner stands about eight feet away from you. Your partner begins to walk toward you speaking a request such as, "I really need you to come to my home and help me get my house organized."

Choose one or all three centers and then say, "Stop." Have your partner notice how this lands on her and then have her guess which center(s) the message came from.

Debrief: Here are a few extra questions to feed this practice:

- Where do you usually speak from?
- Where do you speak from when you are *angry*?

- Where do you speak from when you are *sad*?

- Where do you speak from when you are *happy*?

* *Here are some additional practices for you to explore some fascinating nonverbal sides of the messages we send from our various centers.*

Part F

1. Repeat A, B, C, D and E—this time using only body language. Use hand gestures to signal to your partner when to approach and when to stop.

2. Debrief. What did you notice?

Part G (This one is tougher.)

1. Repeat A, B, C, D and E, but this time see if you can do it all without voice, hand gestures, or body language.

2. Debrief. *What did you notice?*

If your heart is large enough to envelop your adversaries, you can see right through them and avoid their attacks. And once you envelop them, you will be able to guide them along the path indicated to you by heaven and earth.

Morhei Ueshiba, Founder of Aikido

CHAPTER EIGHT

Skillful Vulnerability

W hen I was a kid, I loved reading Superman comics and dreamed of being "invulnerable." Of course, Superman was powerless against a green substance called kryptonite and became a mess around the perplexing love of his life, Lois Lane. Superman's invulnerability came at a cost—a solitary and secretive life that lacked satisfying relationships. Protecting ourselves is sometimes wise, but not if it is at the expense of isolating ourselves.

Vulnerability is rarely seen as something we aspire to achieve. It is highly underrated in our culture. However, being vulnerable is how we allow others to share the power in the beauty of our hearts. It is how we can share our inner spark, our superpower! Vulnerability transmits our wholeness and is the source of our most nurturing connection.

In my trainings, I witness time and again the draw created when someone who is scared or shy reaches past his or her fears and wounded-ness to connect with others in the circle. To the extent that our chronic protective mechanisms keep others out, we lose access to those internal resources we are so dearly protecting. The task is to discern which of these protective strategies serve us and which don't (and with whom). Then we can begin developing present-day strategies for separating real from imagined dangers and staying vulnerable at appropriate moments and in the right measure.

Recent neurological studies show that when someone physically enters your personal space, you map them in your brain and actually perceive them as becoming part of you. Skillful vulnerability attends to our personal space and guides us so we can safely and skillfully expand it to include others. This chapter contains empathic listening visualizations and ideas for re-framing boundaries into places where one touches and encounters others rather than walls to keep others out. Thus, boundaries become empathic faculties that regulate and monitor your personal space, fostering connection while providing greater safety.

Listening to another emphatically triggers our own emotional responses. Just as the iris regulates how much light the eye needs, in relationship we can learn to notice what is too much or too little for our systems to process. Once we notice ourselves becoming overwhelmed, we can self-regulate how much we are willing to take in. The more we practice and reclaim our empathic faculties, the more we pick up from others. Learning how to regulate what we receive and release are critical skills. Centering practices offer a way to build tolerance for such emotions, take full responsibility for their arising, and change our relationships to them.

Space as a Resource

In the Judeo-Christian religions there is a time designated each week that encourages us to take some space to appreciate our being-ness. It is called the Sabbath. When a Jewish boy or girl turns 13, they can participate in a coming of age ritual that for a boy is called a bar mitzvah and for a girl, a bat mitzvah. The centerpiece of this rite of passage is when the young person stands in front of the community, shares personal insights on that week's Torah portion, and is received and valued for the first time as an adult member of the community. Everyone listens as the young adult reads and sings from the ancient Hebrew text in the Torah, Judaism's holiest of scriptures. The young adult's unique perspective is recognized as necessary for the whole community to progress deeper. The task is to find new understanding in these ancient wisdom texts that is relevant to our lives now.

When my son Sam spoke to the community that gathered at his bar mitzvah, he said that in his portion of the Torah, it was written and translated that God said, "If you do not keep the Sabbath, you will be put to death." At that point, Sam stepped to the side of the podium, rested his elbow on it, and spoke intimately with his audience. He confessed: "For most of my 13 years, I almost never kept the Sabbath. Since I am standing here, alive and well, there must be something more to it than the literal translation." He continued: "The way I figure it, I'm a pretty good tap dancer, and when I don't pay attention to the space in between the steps, I can rush the beats that I make with my feet, and that can really kill the dance. Somehow, paying attention to the space helps me keep the rhythm.

"There are people in my life who seem to work constantly trying to make ends meet, to pay their mortgages, and put us kids through school. They work hard to be secure. Sometimes I get caught up in that habit of working constantly, too. What I've noticed is that when I forget to appreciate who I am in the space between what I am doing, life can get pretty mixed up. So what I think my Torah portion is about is the importance of remembering to appreciate what matters, what it is that makes life worthwhile. To me, the meaning of Sabbath is this: If we live without paying attention to the space between all that we are doing, we'll choke the life out of our being. And whether it's a Friday evening, or any other moment of the day or week, the space between all that we do is where we must remember to connect to life, to who we are and what matters."

"Debussy, the great French modern classical composer described music as the space between the notes." Is space just empty and full of nothing? Quantum physics suggests that space is something that we can enliven by our own thoughts and intentions. Space is paradoxical. It can be a lonely place or a place of communion. The space on top of a mountain can touch us in ways that lends perspective to the immensity of our oneness. There is the magical space in the dark starry sky casting its spell over the whole earth. There are the many spaces that intertwine in an ancient forest that invite us to breathe in a sense of awe and feel loved. It is as if each thing in its particularity merges into and connects through the space in and around us.

Within the pause, a Sabbath, at any moment, is where intuition may arise and inspiration occurs. Maybe in the space between our words and actions is the Life we all share. We are immersed in an energetic field that can be sensed intuitively, felt as warmth, or even measured with scientific equipment as electromagnetism. This field connects each of us to the world. It informs our choices. It can say to others "go away" or "come closer." While you cannot fully control the timing of life's experiences or other people's words and actions, you do have some say about the quality and influence of your own space.

Ma-ai

A basic skill to master in Aikido is utilizing *ma-ai*. *Ma* translates as space or interval and *ai* as confluence or joining. Ma-ai is the study and control of the distance in time and space between things. Ma-ai is an optimal critical distance between everything from planets and stars to cells and the molecules in our bodies. Simply put, it is the art of being in the right place at the right time, not too close and not too far. In the world of Aikido if you are too far away, you cannot engage well; too close, and you become inefficient and open to attack. When two master swordsmen square off, their attention tunes into the electrically charged emotional vibrations in the empty space. They read one another to sense any opening in the other's defense. Understanding ma-ai invites each to move the instant before the enemy's response. Artists of every medium know how the emptiness and vacuum of space, used well, can grab attention, draw, repel, and evoke emotional responses. The masters of good phrasing, like the fine martial artist, are people who pay attention to the pauses and silence surrounding and within the action.

Applying this lesson to our own lives, ma-ai means to appreciate and develop a good sense of timing in human affairs, becoming aware of one another's space and learning how to adjust to various conditions. It also teaches us to create and maintain a connection across the space between us.

Incorporating *ma-ai* in the art of living expands the realm of perception, insight, and intuition. Rather than filling the space, it might mean creating the pause to assess, adjust, and correct our stances according to the demands of our daily lifestyles. It is an active inactivity. In our busy lives, we don't leave room for empty spots and contemplative moments for doing nothing. As Sam shared, a pause is not a lack of music; it is an integral part of the composition. In regard to empathy, there is great value in not cluttering up the space with words and learning to get out of the way so the space can inform us. This invites a reinterpretation of boundaries that allows, listens, and ensures the necessary space needed to maximize our chances for harmony.

Reinterpreting Boundaries

In the moment when boundaries touch boundaries, actions trigger reactions, and self-talk intensifies. Boundaries are places where we meet. How we frame them provides us with choices as to whether we connect and include or disconnect and exclude.

In the *old* paradigm, boundaries are emotional or physical walls we put in place to protect ourselves, the more impenetrable the better. We construct boundaries through rules and regulations that are meant to unilaterally control others, especially children, as well as to protect us from others' aggression. When boundaries are imposed on us, it is natural to want to break them down. Aggressor/victim behaviors are logical extensions of the boundary-setting strategies of this paradigm.

In the *new* paradigm, when boundaries touch, they become meeting places, outposts for gathering information for making intuitive choices, checkpoints at the perimeter of our personal space. These boundaries are permeable. They are sentries to screen and filter what we do or don't want to allow in physically, emotionally, verbally, and energetically. Framed this way, boundaries are shock absorbers. They are choice makers. Boundaries help us to discern what is too much for us to take in and manage at any given moment and help us assess what is or isn't a real danger.

Each feeling we have limits emotional energy and allows it to be experienced. It is almost impossible to allow ourselves to be vulnerable with others when we're triggered and in pain. It is important to know and set limits. Emotional pain is a contracted state. Empathy is a physically expansive and vulnerable state of being.

Centering helps make some space, still our internal chatter, and open us more to another's reality and what they are expressing. This doesn't necessarily mean that we agree with their reality. It's simply a practice of accepting what is true for them.

Understanding on an interpersonal level is found by listening clearly to what another is saying or, contrariwise, to be heard clearly by others. Learning to observe without evaluating and judging, a core skill of NVC, supports understanding that opens our ability to see beyond the misapprehension of a circumstance and find a deeper truth to what is really taking place. The harvest of understanding—common ground—is not self-serving, but prompts us to serve others. Understanding does not make a situation go away; it points us toward a deeper path and response.

Shifting old internal patterns and reactions begins with turning inward to accept and serve ourselves in the same way. Self-acceptance is the process of understanding why and how our core strategies were established in the first place and, in doing so, uncovers a preciousness that moves us and touches others.

ATTENTION PRACTICES

Core Attention

Core attention brings us more fully into our centers, connects us to our periphery, and gives us the best possible chance of connecting to another's center from where our boundaries touch.

As in the S.U.R.F. Practice, imagine a bubble that extends a few feet all around you—above, below, front, back, and to your sides. You are   in its center. This bubble is your shock absorber, the first point of contact with all that comes in contact with you. If engaged, the ride will be less bumpy.

These two circles represent two individuals meeting at the peripheries of their personal space, a

few feet from each other's physical body (the dots). Aikido training teaches the value of staying connected, especially through adversity. There is an old saying, "Keep those you love close, and keep your enemies closer." In any interaction, the more skillful you become, the better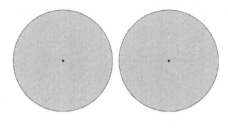
you can learn to utilize whatever connection you have, even if the connection is very small. Bumping up against another can knock you off your center. It's hard to think straight when we don't feel safe. Actually monitoring the space around us helps us discern whether we are truly physically safe or not. When we know our basic needs for safety are met, we become more relaxed, and with that comes more awareness.

A Core Attention Practice

We'll start with a shortened version of the Locating Core Contraction Practice (page 69). Have someone stand 8 to 10 feet away from you (or, if you are alone you can imagine someone is there). Imagine this person is someone you have never met, . . . possibly a stranger who is walking up to you on the street. As this unknown presence moves closer, notice any places that tighten, any rushes of energy, new sensations, pain, changes of internal temperature, shifts in breathing patterns, or any other physical responses.

When a stranger comes too close, it can be felt. When we do not feel safe, it is especially hard, almost impossible, to be empathetic. One can adjust the distance in order to relax, think more clearly, and possibly avert danger.

Now begin the practice again. At the moment you begin to feel that the other person is at the edge of your personal space and too close for comfort, say "Stop!" and then drop your attention to the core of your body. Notice any sensations, tightness, and/or contractions. Center, relax, and assess whether you are safe or not by discerning what your sensations are trying to tell you to do next.

Now take a step and move in a way that relaxes your system, most likely a step back or to the side. As the other person takes another step toward you, feel your internal landscape, then move and adjust to a distance that feels safe. Regardless of whether there is a true threat, you will somatically experience the unknown presence touching your space as threatening. This is part of your hardwiring. The body doesn't know what is real and what is imagined. It will react in ways it has practiced most when a threat is perceived. The tension felt in the position and distance between people is a nonverbal factor that impacts conversations in positive and negative ways all the time. The more you notice such impacts, the more consciously you can learn to work with them.

Empathic Attention

Centering yourself expands your field to give you more ground and makes room for others. This diagram represents empathic listening. By maintaining a centered presence, you can stabilize your "listening field," then expand it to include others graciously. Although we are not responsible for what another person feels, we can be mindful of our own physical and nonphysical touch.

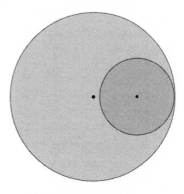

Empathic listening helps inform us when physical touch is appropriate and when it is not. Sometimes physical touch, like words, can get in the way of empathy. Empathy is not about trying to change others. We can ask ourselves how high, deep, and wide must I be with another, and then adjust. If we can hold the space above, below, and around the other as intensely as the feelings flowing from our hearts, we can love in a compassionate way. Balancing our own field without attachment or resistance allows an unimpeded, creative movement to any part of the interaction. Communicating one thing with words and something else by the quality of our presence can be confusing and sometimes damaging. When we center and open our attention to hold others with care, they are drawn into our calmness and stability. This also affords us the best vantage point from which to read their intentions, as well as to gauge distances that feel safe or not. This is how skillful vulnerability fosters connection, greater safety, and good timing.

EMPATHIC ATTENTION PRACTICE

Imagine the space around and within you is more than just emptiness—that it is a medium through which comprehensive communication and empathy are transmitted.

1. Stand or sit at arm's length from your partner so the periphery of your personal space touches the periphery of your partner's. (Both arms fully extended, tips of fingers touching one another's.)

2. As in the S.U.R.F. Centering practice imagine your personal space as a bubble extending a couple feet all around you. At first let it gently bump up to your partner's personal space. Take a moment to fill your space with an intention of kindness, gratitude, or appreciation.

3. Slowly expand this field of attention (bubble) to include the other's bubble.

4. Open and hold this field for 30 seconds and just listen, even if words are not being spoken.

5. Disengage and reflect silently for 30 seconds.

6. Hold this listening field for 1 minute.

7. Disengage and reflect silently for 30 seconds.

8. Hold this listening field for 2 minutes.

9. Disengage and reflect silently for 30 seconds.

A somatic inquiry

How was it to be held? Here, recount any feelings, stories, and sensations that came up. How was it for you to hold someone in this way? Again relate your feelings, stories, and sensations, both comfortable and uncomfortable.

- Now begin again, and this time, once you have included the other in the quality of your listening field for about 30 seconds, each of you share something the other person does not know about you.

- Try this with a few other qualities, such as kindness, gratitude, integrity, or grace.

- Appreciate what your partner says, and then share how the quality of your listening affected the conversations.

Merged Attention

Merged attention occurs when you lose your own center and believe that your feelings and needs are the responsibility of another. In this diagram, merged attention is represented as an oval with no true center. In this state, with two quasi-centers, it is hard to discern who is who in the interaction. In this state, blaming and shaming are common. Merged attention can be seductive and cause a lot of pain and confusion when we get drawn into the dramas of those around us and then lose ourselves and even base our self-importance on the other.

A MERGED ATTENTION PRACTICE

Find a partner and in a role-play, set up a conflict between the two of you so that it is filled with blame and judgments of one another. Make this power-over, oppressor/victim scenario a 2 or 3 on a scale of 1 to 10, with 10 being the most intense. Let the argument go on for a minute or so

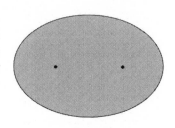

and then notice how you feel. Do either of you have a clear sense of your needs? Are you feeling fully responsible for your emotions? Do you feel centered?

Harmonizing Attention

Both merging and harmonizing have a moment of empathy. The difference is that with harmonizing attention, your sense of autonomy remains intact. This is a state in which you and others are in sync, together in a moment, and recognize that your deepest needs are the same. In this state, what is there to resist? When there are two of us, and you see me as different, it is easy to want to attack, but in harmonizing attention, there is no longer an attacker and a defender. In this diagram of harmonized attention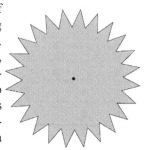

there is no center as a reference point. Athletes know it as being "in the zone"—a moment of peak performance where self and other become one. It is a powerful state in which one's training kicks in. Sometimes it's just pure creativity and no longer about trying but about letting go. This zone is elusive. It is a powerfully creative, present state of being. It is a time of feeling, allowing, and trusting. Once you start thinking about it, become attached to outcomes, or try to stay in it, you lose it.

A HARMONIZING ATTENTION PRACTICE

In this practice, the instructions are for one person as he or she holds the other in a healing field of attention.

Core Attention: Give yourself a moment to breathe deeply, drop your attention into your core, and let yourself relax. Notice the person who is in front of you. Focus your senses on him or her (for simplicity, from here on, I will speak of "him").

With your eyes, notice his appearance. Are you drawn, or do you feel that you want to move away? Notice visually colors and textures. Invite your curiosity to any response your body has to what you see. This person is speaking through his body, giving information that you can sense...as long as you decide to *care*.

Expand your field of empathic attention to include your partner.

As this new relationship takes shape, breathe, relax, and receive any words that are spoken to you and just let them pass through you. To listen and receive in this way may invite some pain to arise. Notice whether you are willing to feel, receive, and accept any pain. Are you willing to care? Do you want to be of service?

Just receive the pain and allow this relationship to form. *How you intuitively respond to his pain will give you information about its nature as it reveals much about your own.*

Now start to bring your attention more to the tone and textures of his voice and what is communicated in the sound. Is it flowing or bitter, lyrical and melodic, or monotonous and dreary? Is there life in it? As you listen to his voice, what feelings arise in you?

How is your body in response? Do you breathe easier? Is your heart lighter? Does your chest or jaw tighten? Listen without agenda. Quiet any judgments you may be having and just notice your body as it gives you information about him.

What comes up physically and emotionally for you, and where does it come up in you the most? Do you have the courage of heart to follow your attention where it is taking you? Are you willing to feel what you feel?

Listening in this way might stir up self-judgments about being invasive and staying out of another's business because of things we have been taught about social politeness. Allow such judgments to arise for a moment and then let them pass. Catch and release. Muster courage and care. Use self-honesty to work with any thoughts that tell you that you are bad or wrong for feeling, sensing, or seeing so privately into another or anything that dampens your own awareness.

With empathic listening we get reads on people. These are emotional hits that give a general sense about what in another stands out—a sense of happiness, pain, melancholy, fear, or any other qualities?

Now let yourself begin to care. This requires a generous spirit that is capable of taking in a wide horizon. Do you have a resistance to caring? Be creative, work and allow your awareness to expand and include him as you access your natural ability to love.

Fill your heart and the space around you with a quality such as care or kindness, and then slowly envelope the other in it. With this intention, place your attention on the place that you sense is the most contracted and in pain within you in response to his. Surround this place as you would hold a young child you are calming. Receive its communications to your heart. Send your kindness back in response as you listen for the source of the pain in his body, its unique voice. Let any resistance just pass through you or go off to another part of your awareness to find understanding in its own way. Just listen with the intention to see.

Harmonizing Attention: Breathe, be present and patient. From your centered awareness, distinct and unique, feel the life that moves through both of you, intersecting and weaving to understand. This is a deep empathy.

Our innate powers for healing and connection have been with us since the beginning and have not diminished, no matter how unaware of them we may be as we navigate our modern, technologically oriented world. Every single one of us knows suffering, and from our wounds we also find our wholeness and the wisdom for how to heal. Deeply present listening between all beings in our human and nonhuman community may be the most tangible step we can take toward healing our collective wounds.

Ultimately because of our connection and interdependence, we know on a deep level that our actions in life must love beyond knowing.

Wendell Berry

CHAPTER NINE

Responsible Self

Core Participation

My neighbor Carolyn is a Native American elder. She and I were in a cere-
monial sweat lodge that my son and his fiancé called for support
and blessings as their wedding day approached. In the sweat lodge, when you
offer words, you end what you say by respectfully uttering "*Mitákuye
Oyás'in*"—a phrase from the Lakota language that reflects their world-view of
interconnect- edness. The phrase translates as "all my relatives," "we are all
related," or "all my relationships." It is a prayer of oneness and harmony with all
forms of life: ancestors, people, animals, birds, insects, trees, plants, rivers,
mountains, valleys, and even rocks.

When it was Carolyn's turn to speak, she said: "One morning I walked out
to my backyard, and I looked at all the plants and the nature around me, and I
waved my hands as I said, "*Mitákuye* Oyás'iŋ." I noticed that as I waved,
everything around me was like a blur of green, as when a queen waves at her
subjects and sees a blur of faces. This particular day, I walked out, and there
was this tree, and I thought, "I'm not even sure what kind of tree you are. I
don't know anything about you. If you are my relation, then we are in
relationship. And if I'm
in a relationship with you, what is my responsibility? You're supplying oxygen.
You're holding my hillside together. You're doing all kinds of things for me that
I'm not even aware of, and you're in the natural flow of divine Grace, and I am
here sitting and doing the queen's wave thinking I'm connected to you—but I'm
not. So what is my responsibility to you?"

The Lakota language is an action-oriented language. "*Mitákuye* Oyás'iŋ," interpreted as "all my relationships", is a call to act responsibly. Carolyn, realizing that relationship is a two-way street, said: "I thought that going out to my yard every day and making that announcement engaged me. I thought I was in sync with the flow. But I was just standing on the bank waiting as the river was rushing by."

It is easy to fool ourselves into thinking we are responsible and engaged, only to find—upon deeper reflection—that we are practicing many forms of disconnection. Commitment and participation in relationships must come from a deep hunger, from the core of our beings. We are either bystanders or we're in the mix. Active engagement that begins from our core is the commitment. In all relationships, the extent to which we can wholeheartedly participate is the extent to which we can know ourselves.

Paradoxology 101

We dehydrate food so it becomes light and easy to carry in our backpacks. When it is time to eat, we rehydrate it so it becomes delicious to eat. Marshall Rosenberg's NVC dehydrates basic building blocks of relationship, making them incredibly accessible. It is up to those of us who carry on this body of work to reinvigorate the work and make it our own through creativity and consciousness. Marshall, in his creation of NVC, offered a brilliant process for growing healthy relationships.

At first watching Marshall Rosenberg in action, his processes seemed elusive— hardly linear and almost magical. He was consistently dynamic and present when listening and communicating with individuals. He often stated that the processes were the map and not the territory, which alluded to the paradoxical nature of relationship and learning. Being creative with NVC requires us, over time, to allow what we have practiced and embodied to emerge. As we come into the essence of relationships, paradoxes emerge. Here is where we are given both loving connection and solitude. It is like a painter surrendering to his canvas and inspiration. To walk into the mystery of relationship requires us to recognize paradox in those circular arguments where each has important things to say and neither has the whole picture. It takes skill to identify what the conflict is there to reveal.

Know/Don't Know

To quiet the enemy images we project onto others and listen more intuitively, empathic communication requires taking responsibility for our own moods, emotions, thoughts, and feelings. Between asking the question and receiving the information, empathy is a state of openness, resonance, and not knowing. Paradoxically, being open to "not knowing" allows inner wisdom, guidance, and direction to arise.

In school, right answers get rewards. Wrong answers get low marks and criticism. In traditional education, we are not generally taught that mystery is an exciting part of learning. I am not speaking of the kind of mystery commonly understood as something we need to find an answer to, as in a good mystery novel. I am referring to the mystery that, by its very nature, is unsolvable—the unknown realms in which we live. This kind of Mystery has power. It is human to feel discomfort with what you don't know, and there are always unknowns.

In 1985, when I completed my apprenticeship as a goldsmith, I sold all my belongings, said goodbye to everyone, donned a backpack, and left to travel for the next three and a half years. One does not, however, need to leave home to be a traveler. Being a traveler is a state of mind that recognizes each one of us as part of a global family and an unfathomable universe. Therefore, there is always much we can learn about one other. Throughout my travels, I carried two questions that speak to a central paradox in human relationship:

How are we different? How are we the same?

These questions remain with me as I share my trainings around the world with people of all ages and walks of life. Honoring both our uniqueness and our commonality is foundational for healthy relationships. Paradoxes that are unrecognized can be the source of a lot of pain and confusion. We want a sense of safety and belonging, while paradoxically we want to find excitement and freedom. We wish to rest in the security of being loved, while we are pulled by desire and the intrigue of something mysterious and different. Desire seeks the safety of love, while love seeks the mystery of desire. Moving between and holding such polarities is a core skill for deepening relationships.

Muhammad Ali, the great boxing champion, addressed a central paradox when he stood in front of the 1975 Harvard graduating class and was asked to recite one of his original poems, perhaps the shortest one ever written. It went like this:

"Me, We!"

Learning to hold the paradox of "me" and "we" as separate and intersecting is also the radical insight of modern depth psychology and a core principle found in wisdom traditions around the world. The ancient Hindu writing, the Upanishads, speak of an individual self and a greater universal Self that are separated only by illusion created in our minds. A central prayer in Judaism, the Shema, begins with a line that roughly translates as, "Listen, you who wrestles with Spirit, the spirit that is knowable and the unknowable Spirit are one. "Buddha, at the end of his seven-year quest, in the moment he attained enlightenment under the Bodhi tree, had a choice of being one with the universe or coming back to the human realm in order to serve and guide. He chose to be a model of the individual who serves within the collective from powerful self-knowing.

The practice of seeing paradoxically builds the capacity to love others even when we are upset and angry with them. Narrow-minded moralities with judgments that promote "us vs. them" strategies take root when paradox is not considered. And still, without duality, nothing makes sense. We know left because we know right; we know gentle because we know harsh; sweet because we know bitter; joy because we know sorrow. We know "me" because we know "we." Although we see through our individual eyes, we also dream collective dreams, see through group eyes, through class eyes, through ethnic eyes. In addition, we communicate through language and conceptual thinking rooted in collective realities.

Autonomy/Mutuality

At first, an infant's perception is a sense of interbeing: mother and child are one. The idea of "interbeing" is a word introduced by Thich Nhat Hanh into the North American Buddhist vocabulary to describe our "dependent co-arising", not just of mother and child but in regards to all life. Gradually, we crawl away from our parents, and autonomy develops out of our earlier mutual consciousness. Individuality is an important achievement, but not the ultimate destination. In our cultural frontier stories that glorify the individual who needs no one, the goal of self-sufficiency obscures the essential next stage of human development: maturing as a centered, stabilizing, contributing individual within the collective to which we have always belonged. A healthy child's autonomy grows out of, but does not replace, group and family consciousness. Instead, our individual and collective consciousness necessarily operate and evolve in tandem. Those who have established a healthy sense of this mutuality/autonomy paradox are more able to express their likes, dislikes, and choices and to accept the consequences of their actions. Wendell Berry said it this way, "There is no such thing as independence, only responsible and irresponsible dependence." Carl Rogers, the father of humanistic psychology, articulated his understanding this way: "Before every session I take a moment to remember my humanity, that there is no experience that this man has that I cannot share with him, no fear that I cannot understand, no suffering that I cannot care about, because I too am human. No matter how deep his wounds, he does not need to be ashamed in front of me. I too am vulnerable. And because of this, I am enough. Whatever his story, he no longer needs to be alone with it. This is what will allow his healing to begin."

The Personal and the Empathic Self

Marshall Rosenberg, in his inimitable, simple, and entertaining teaching style, gives voice to our dual nature and inner schism with two puppets—a jackal and a giraffe. I understand the jackal to represent the landscape of the "personal self," filled with memories, learned familiar and cultural patterns, perceptions, ideas, relationships, exchanges, hurts, gifts, and fears of the unknown, while the giraffe represents the greater landscape—beyond the personal—that part of us that swims in the deeper ocean of relatedness. I this call our "empathic self." The personal and empathic selves are two sides of the same coin. Learning to appreciate and hold them in tandem is a key to authenticity. To forsake either damages us.

The Empathic Self

It's difficult to talk about things you cannot measure, touch, or factually account for, even if these things are probably the most real and common to us all. Rosenberg's giraffe character was picked for two main qualities: it has the largest heart of any land animal and, being so tall, it has purview over a wide horizon. The giraffe character represents how we are when we are centered in our hearts and in touch with our highest values. I like the term empathic self to describe this "giraffe-ness" in less whimsical terms because empathy, being the "language of the heart," connects us to all other hearts. William Blake said, "There is only one Heart." Empathy is how we can fathom our wholeness and unity with all life...in a moment. It connects us to the data bank of life, what Carl Jung called the collective unconscious, where we can access the wisdom to act personally and think globally.

Since the heart does not habituate, listening empathically connects us to the present moment. Rather than a way of thinking, our empathic self relates more to a way of being and grace. The empathic self, like a caring elder is the part of us that can accept our fallibility, mortality, and interdependence. It's our conscious compass to check in with when life knocks us off center. We're not built to be in this state more than a small fraction of the time. To be there too long can overload our systems. Bruce Lee, one of the most celebrated martial artists, explained it this way, "It's not about being centered all the time, it is about knowing when you are off and training to come back quicker."

Personal Self

Fears and feelings can run you ragged. Living in fear of the unknown leads to orchestrating a controlled paint by number life set up to avoid any surprises as much as possible. However, any way of ordering life, artistically, socially, economically, or politically is incomplete.

I like to think of Marshall Rosenberg's jackal in a similar vein as Coyote in Native American tales, whose mischievous ways always stir things up. He is the trickster who always shows up unexpectedly, usually following his hungry belly or some emotional urge. The mythical Coyote is a divine messenger that, like emotions, can shake you up and, in the process, reveal parts of yourself most in need of attention. Like Coyote, your personal self, when faced with the unknowns of life and love, can be harsh and judgmental, obsessing over who's right or wrong, grasping for the concrete proof of things, fearful of scarcity or loss.

This jackal part of us is an integral part of our personality that adds dimension, tension, and color.

Your personal self's bumps and missteps, re-framed through your empathic self, can become a tap on the shoulder from a helping friend. By honoring the personal and the empathic self *together*, habits, superstitions, self-limiting preconceptions, prejudgments, methodologies, and patterns of speech become more apparent. This awareness is a step toward positive changes.

Facing the rifts in relationships begins and ends with facing our inner schisms—the bright and shiny sides that we want the world to see and the shadow sides that we keep hidden and out of sight. On some level, whatever we try to cover up, others feel. Mistrust is felt when our words are not in sync with our feelings and intentions. Conversely, the more of you that you bring to the table, the more others trust and feel your authenticity. Living in fear of the unknown can lead to orchestrating a controlled life that sets things up to avoid surprises as much as possible. With practice, holding our personal and empathic selves in tandem, we can tolerate our feelings more and more and appreciate the mystery one step at a time.

Vulnerability and transparency are the fertile grounds for seeing one another through the lens of the heart and to see, as Ram Dass so succinctly put it, "I am that too."

Authenticity

Head (thoughts), heart (feelings), and belly (intuition) alignment is the basis for actions that transmit power and authenticity. Conversely, internal dissonance transmits mixed messages. We have our personal fears, shadows, quirks, and gifts against the backdrop of our empathic self that knows the big picture, that "to love another is to love your self." Holding both aspects of our self with appreciation in tandem builds the capacity to receive and express love. Together, they say, "Yes, I am struggling in this relationship, and I am willing to go deeper for the sake of love." "Yes, I am angry that I got a reprimand from my boss, and I can appreciate his desire for efficiency." Our personal self says, "No, I am too sleepy to play with you right now." Our empathic self says, "*And* I would enjoy playing after a nap when I am more rested."

The personal self is afraid of loss and needs to find answers. The empathic self trusts that life will reveal its meaning as we quiet to listen from a centered place. In conflict, the goal is not to be our empathic selves all the time; it is to learn to come back to center so we can create an empathic connection more quickly and train to sustain it longer. Sustaining a centered, empathic state just one second more before reacting opens huge possibilities for more compassionate and effective strategies to enter. Between another's actions and our responses, there is a space with infinite possibilities.

Our empathic and personal selves together are who we are. The point is to translate our reactive messages through empathy into heartfelt and comprehensive strategies again and again. This will move us toward what feeds our souls, such as kindness and trust.

Response-ability

Taking responsibility for our actions supports movement toward self-empow- erment and having relationships free from blame and guilt. Being responsible recognizes that we are all in this together, that how we respond to life profoundly affects others—most likely in more ways than we can calculate. There are many speech patterns that do not support us in taking personal responsibility for our actions, such as "I have to..." or "I will get in trouble if I..." or "I can't because..." Another way to obscure personal responsibility comes in statements that assign responsibility for our feelings to someone else and contain an air of victim-hood by implying that things are out of our control, such as: "She made me feel so angry!" or "You make me so mad."

Some other ways we give up personal responsibility:

- Personal diagnosis - "I overeat because I am depressed."
- Actions of others - "I spank my child because he talked back to me."
- Group pressure - "Everyone else smokes—that's why I do."
- Institutional policies and regulations - "Those are the rules. There is nothing I can do."
- Impulse - "I had to eat that cake."

- Gender, social, or age roles - "Well, you know how guys are..."

We have so many outside influences that we allow to imprison our thoughts. Try this:

1. Write down something you are telling yourself you have to do or that you have no choice about.

2. Now write what it is you are worried would happen if you stop doing the thing you're telling yourself you have to do.

In addition, when someone says, "You make me feel...(angry, sad, hurt, etc.)," most likely they are attempting to blame you for what they are feeling. Whenever you hear or use this phrase: "You make me feel..." *pause and remember* that other people may be the stimulus of your feelings, but they are not the cause. Our feelings are caused by our reactions to situations (our thoughts and judgments about what happened) and by our unmet needs in that moment. In fact, the same stimulus (circumstances can elicit very different feelings in us at different times depending on what we are needing in that moment—how stressed or tired we are, for example, or a host of other factors that may be in play.

The guideline here is to pay attention to the deeper motivations that lead you to choose the actions you take. Take care to distinguish between your thoughts and feelings. When you need to express your feelings, be sure to use feeling words as you actually feel what you are feeling in order to not transmit moral judgments or criticism. We are each responsible for our own feelings."

AN AUTHENTICITY PRACTICE

How do you feel when someone talks to you with loving words, even though you can feel his or her unexpressed anger? How do you feel when someone is upset and unleashes their honest feelings and judgments about you unchecked? Both these scenarios leave in their wake an uneasy feeling that the other shoe is about to drop. Others feel our authenticity when we vulnerably and honestly reveal

ourselves. When we express honesty and empathy in "tandem—others experience our authenticity. Authenticity also holds what we know(our empathic self) and what we don't know(our personal self) in tandem. Although we might not know what will happen or what we will do next, we can know the qualities of being we choose to live by.

Set up a role-play with a friend or partner around a difficulty you are having in a particular relationship. On a scale of 1 to 10, first choose a situation with an emotional charge of about 2 or 3. The Speaker and Receiver stand a couple of feet apart and face one another. The Speaker then acts out what is upsetting as if the Receiver were the actual person the Speaker is angry with.

First Scenario

1. Speaker: Express your thoughts and emotions, unchecked. Let your personal self run with all your judgments.

Example of personal self (what you don't know): "I don't know what to do about this. I am so upset that I have to ask you again and again to PUT YOUR CLOTHES AWAY!! Take care of it."

2. Receiver: Pay attention to the sensations in your body and notice how you feel being spoken to in this way.

Second Scenario

1. Speaker: Identify what you care about, your needs, and then speak to the Receiver while keeping the anger or hurt emotions you feel just below the surface to yourself.

Example: Empathic self (what you do know): (speaking sweetly with hidden anger) I need to have some order in this house, and I feel sad and frustrated when I come home and your clothes are all over the living room. Will you please clean your things up?"

2. Receiver: Notice how you feel when you are spoken to in this way.

* Keep in mind that the empathic self when centered is quite connective. The difficulty is that in real situations, it is hard to center. The next scenario is a real time transition, centering in motion from triggered to centered and present.

Third Scenario

1. Speaker: Start by first speaking about what is bothering you (personal) and then ground your statement by identifying and including the deeper needs (empathic), such as honesty, integrity, connection, consideration, etc. Make sure the connecting word is an "and," not a "but." **Example:** (with frustration) "Sam, I get so angry seeing your dirty clothes all over the place, and I don't know what to do about it, (slightly less pained) *and* what matters to me is finding respectful ways to talk and live together. (With respect, say) Would you please keep your dirty clothes out of our common living areas?"

2. Receiver: Pay attention to the sensations in your body and notice how you feel when you are spoken to in this way.

Did you notice a difference?

The personal self will hide our vulnerability; hang on to stories, habits, and beliefs; and grasp for footholds. The personal self is also highly motivated to make things better. Through practice, we can learn to push the override button, re-center, acknowledge our personal self, and not beat ourselves up doing it. The empathic self connects us to our whole being. When both are engaged and present, nothing is hidden, and this is what can build trust on many levels.

There once were two frogs that fell into two buckets of cream. The walls of the pails were too steep to climb. The first frog swam around and around and around and eventually gave up and drowned. The second frog also swam around and around and around but refused to give up until finally it was sitting on a mound of butter.

This story of the frogs reminds me of a central practice in Aikido called *Irimi Tenkan*. Both are about choice and turning toward life. Irimi Tenkan translates from Japanese to "enter and turn." It is a foundational Aikido movement that is both easy to learn and wonderfully complex to explore.

A PRACTICE OF DIGNITY

Dignity is a quality of authenticity that others feel from someone who is responsible for their choices and actions. Physically it is an alignment of self, the ground you stand on, and your highest knowing. Entering adulthood, having and raising children, marriage, as well as many stages in long-term relationships and aging, are some of the more pronounced thresholds we step across where something gets left behind in order to discover what we are on our way to becoming. Such transitions always renew my appreciation of Aikido as a warrior training in love and courage.

Entering and facing life "upright"—with your head, heart, and belly aligned—is a shape of authentic dignity. Common sense is demonstrated in the movements *irimi* and *tenkan*. We naturally do *irimi tenkan* in everyday life without thinking. Imagine walking down a crowded street as someone is walking directly toward you. To avoid colliding, you may quickly back up, but then you might inadvertently bump into someone walking behind you. Common sense says to continue to walk toward him and perhaps step slightly to the side to let him pass by, then continue on your way, much like the toreador who steps to the side and leads the charging bull to pass. This is *irimi*. If you loose your balance, you would not grab the person, much less a bull, and cling to steady yourself. Instead, you might turn on your axis to keep your balance and then keep walking. This is *tenkan*. As you meet the person on the street who is walking toward you, your movements thoughtfully and intentionally respond, rather than conflict with them. The meeting and interaction between you and the pedestrian become a continuous and smooth flow of give and take, force and direction that initiates unity.

Irimi is about inquiry. If you are afraid of something, learn about it. The practice of *irimi* can be used to work with internal conflicts as well as external aggression.

Tenkan is centering in motion. Like a top, the vertical axis becomes more obvious as the spinning movement helps inform you if your center of balance is true or not. Aikido students train to receive force and transform it to become a helper
rather than to fight it. In both *irimi* and *tenkan* we enter and face our fears in an honest and skillful way. In doing so, change is invited to occur. Aikido teaches boundaries, yet insists on closeness. One must be willing to meet and blend with the attacker's energy in order to feel where and how you can lead it.

The Practice

First practice stepping and turning back and forth until the movement of the practice begin to feel fluid. Keep in mind as you enter and turn to:

ï   Remain level headed. Don't bounce.

ï   Stay relaxed and flexible—not too stiff and not too loose.

ï   Breathe fully and deeply as you move.

ï   Move with intention and the qualities you are training in.

ï   Focus beyond what you are facing—out toward the horizon.

ï   You are always entering. Don't drift backward after you turn.

ï   Minimize extraneous movement.

Here are some elements you might consider at every stage of this movement:

Face: Face with courage of heart what you are choosing. Relax, listen, center, and be open to what is on your path.

Enter: Take a step. *Center and let the motion and space clarify what you are doing and choosing.*

Turn: Breathe and center. Blend and move with what you are engaging. Lose the enemy image of self and other.

Lead: Lead from within, connect with what is in front of you now, and then begin again.

A Somatic Inquiry: As you enter and turn, let what you care about move you. Hold your personal commitment and what it is in deep service to. Let the power of your intention move you.

The most intense conflicts, if overcome, leave behind a sense of security and calm which is not easily disturbed, or else a broken-ness that can hardly be healed. Conversely, it is just these intense conflicts and their conflagration which are needed in order to produce valuable and lasting results.

Carl Jung

CHAPTER TEN

The Spiral Blend Practice

The Spiral Blend practice appeared one day in its early form while I was out jogging with my wife, Judith. We began to argue over a recurring and polarizing topic—our mutual household responsibilities. Judith said: "It really bums me out that I have to clean your mess when I want to take a bath. Why can't you ever rinse the tub when you are done?!"

Typically, I'd remind her of all the times I actually *did* what she said that I *never* do. And then a back and forth would ensue and grow more and more contentious as we became what our sons refer to as "the Bickersons."

On this particular day, as our fight began to escalate, I had the wherewithal to notice the tightening in my chest at the onset of our conflict and took a centering breath. It was then that I remembered *irimi tenkan*, an Aikido move I had practiced countless times in which you physically step out of the way of an attack, then turn to blend with the direction of the attack to create connection, flow, and unity. As Judith's words and message intensified, I stepped from directly in front of her to the side of her, just off the "line of attack." To my surprise, with that small shift in position, her angry words seemed to sail right by me instead of landing on me, as if I had sidestepped a punch. My chest relaxed slightly, I breathed easier, and my mind cleared enough to separate who I was from what Judith was saying. I did so by letting her jog ahead of me a half step more while I took the time and space to center on what matters to me and the ground that I stand on.

I remembered that I value listening with care, speaking honestly, moving with integrity, and graciousness. Although I often fall short of living up to these qualities, they are the qualities I aspire to become in all relationships. Feeling more centered now, I moved just behind Judith's right shoulder, running along, with my heart physically just behind hers. From that perspective, I could look over her shoulder and imagine what she was seeing and feeling. From this vantage, her words no longer seemed to be so much about me, but an expression of her own pain. With no agenda other than to understand the source of her pain, I listened. Her voice rose as she said: "I get so mad when I leave the tub clean for you, and then when I want to take a bath, I have to clean the tub before I even begin drawing my bath. I don't feel thought about or cared for."

From a quieted place in me I asked, "Are you upset because you are wanting to feel like we are...partners in tending our home?" There was silence, and then a "Yes," followed by a pause in the conversation. In a slightly trembling voice, Judith added, "I have been working so much lately, and I need the house to be cleaner and more orderly so I can come home and rest."

I took in what she was saying, let it settle, and then reflected, "Are you saying that home is the place for you to rest and find some sanctuary from our busy lives, and that things like laundry folded and the tub being scrubbed make our home a more restful place for you?"

Judith nodded her head in agreement, and her eyes filled with tears. All of a sudden, we were running, on common ground, listening with empathy and speaking with honesty.

Our conflict faded into developing strategies that might work better for both of us around our home. This was the dawn of the Spiral Blend. If it can work with marital flareups, it can likely help with any conflict you face.

This practice takes only seconds or minutes. We'll explore it slowly at first. I have divided this practice into several parts to be learned sequentially. Once you embody the suggested sequence, it can be dropped in favor of using your intuition to divine which position in the process will benefit you most at any given moment.

1. The Role-Play
2. Stimulus and Cause
3. Core Strategies
4. Self-Regulate
5. Self-Empathy

6. The Dance of Empathy and Honesty
7. Mutual Strategies
8. Internalizing the Practice

Setup

There are two roles in this practice, the Receiver and the Challenger. In the initial setup for the role-play, the Receiver tells the Challenger who he or she is and what triggering things to say. Even in role-playing, old traumas can get re-stimulated very quickly, so move slowly and with care. On a scale of 1 to 10, 10 being the most triggering, set up the confrontation to be a 2 or a 3. It is interesting and important to note that the body does not differentiate between what is real and what is imagined. Your body will react in the ways it has practiced most when you are triggered.

In the role-play, when you are the Challenger, instead of just "playing" the part, actually imagine "being" the person the Receiver is asking you to be. For example, if you are playing your partner's brother, ask yourself what it might be like to be his brother, and try to allow the sense of him to come through you. You may be surprised at how this works and feels and what comes out of your mouth!

Important: One of the challenging but necessary steps in setting up this practice, whether in real life or when role-playing, is to agree on who goes first. Generally in a conflict, both participants are triggered. As you perform this practice, remember, we are slowing things way down, and it is the Receiver who will need to center, ground, self-empathize, and give empathy to the Challenger. In the setup, take a moment to be clear about who is the Receiver and who is the Challenger. Remember to take turns in these roles. Trying to process triggering moments simultaneously can quickly become very messy.

It may take a few starts and restarts to land on who is the most triggered and who is the most capable of giving empathy. Conflicts are never a straight line from here to there. Do not be afraid to start over. There is no wrong in this practice, only learning and getting better.

1. Stimulus and Cause

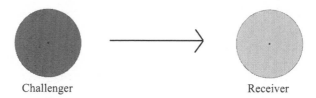

Challenger   Receiver

Challenger: Stand directly in front of the Receiver, point your finger and speak the triggering statement you have been coached to say. For example, "Why don't you ever clean the tub when you are done!" or "I get so angry when you interrupt me all the time." Remember, you are not responsible for another's feelings. You are responsible for your own. It is essential to identify and separate the stimulus(what the Challenger says) from the cause of your pain, your unmet needs in the moment. The feelings that arise provide the clues as to what your needs are.

2. Core Contractions and Strategies

Receiver: As the Challenger's triggering words land on you, drop your attention to locate the center of any tightness, sensation, or emotional pain that is stimulated in your body. This is your core contraction. Ask yourself:

a. Where is there tightness in my body?

b. What are the sensations and where are they strongest?

c. How has my breathing changed?

d. Is there a deadening or an intensifying of emotion anywhere? Where?

Scan your body. Is there anything happening in your chest, shoulders, back, arms, or legs? Bring curiosity and attention to any contractions and sensations you feel. Notice internal stories, judgments, or reactions that surface. At this point, try not to analyze things. Just notice what comes up, and let go of your evaluations.
Catch and release. Describe in detail to your partner what you are experiencing.

Note: If you struggle to locate specifically where the contractions and sensations are in your body—if the triggering seems like everywhere or nowhere—you have probably picked a situation that is more than a 2 or 3 on the scale of 1 to 10. Choose something less intense. The Spiral Blend can help you through these moments as you explore it in depth. I recommend that when first learning this practice, it's good to become familiar with all the facets of the Spiral Blend before you move into more intense role-playing or applications. Everyone has his or her own ways of responding to stress and conflict. Our systems can handle only so much intensity before fight/flight/startle responses kick in and we automatically default to historical, conditioned patterns of behavior. (See Core Strategies, Chapter 5.)

When you are over-stimulated and don't know what to do, move to the next stage of the practice to help relieve your system enough so you can think more clearly and center your attention inward. This will also help you feel and locate your core contractions and core strategies more clearly.

3. Self-Regulate

It is almost impossible to empathize when you are overwhelmed by emotional pain. The more relaxed you are, the more aware you can be and the more you can feel. The more you can feel, the more your emotions can point you toward what you most need in the present moment. When you are relaxed, the people around you relax.

The Wind Practice

Receiver: Moving to the wind position (see pg. 20), step "off the line of attack," and as the Challenger continues to point and speak to your original position, look to see where the words are coming from and then turn your head to follow the Challenger's words and the energy behind them as they pass by you. Don't be fixated on the Challenger; remember to turn your head. After you have watched this train of words go by, turn your head once again to notice where these words originated. This move is much like the toreador who steps effectively and efficiently to the side to let the bull rush by.

Moving to the wind position helps you gain a different perspective on the matter. Step off the line, and keep the same amount of distance between you and the Challenger, taking care not to move farther away or closer to the Challenger. Wind is not about leaving or pushing the interaction. It is about attending to your feelings and getting a fresh perspective while staying connected.

Receiver: In the Wind posture, quietly notice:

a. What sensations do you now feel in your body?
b. How is it different from when you were standing directly on the line of the attack?
c. How do the words land on you now?
d. Does your triggering subside a bit in this new position?
e. Have your feelings or judgments toward the other person changed at all?

4. Self-Empathy

Don't just do something, be here.

Self-empathy is inner listening, where you place the light of your attention on your internal world of feelings, emotions, moods, sensations, and stories that show up in response to life's ups and downs. You must regain a centered sense of who you are and what you care about to put aside your agendas, judgments, or attachments to outcomes—and just listen. This is difficult. Learning to get out of your own way to fully listen is something you can cultivate so you can do it for longer and longer moments. In those moments, your somatic intelligence can point you toward what you need.

1. In the wind position, bring your hands to chest level, with elbows only slightly bent, and your fingers pointed forward. Now vigorously rub your hands together.

2. Reach out. Hold your hands apart and extend your arms and fingers as if you were reaching out to catch a big ball. Notice any tingling of energy in your hands from the friction of rubbing them together.

3. Touch your heart. Bring your palms and their warmth to your heart. Remember and appreciate your heart.

4. Wake up your belly. Now connect your heart to your belly by stroking your torso from your heart down to your belly. Wake up your belly by patting it in the front, the sides and the back. Bring your attention to the center of all that sensation.

5. Ground: Move to ground. With your left foot forward, bend your legs slightly so you feel grounded and centered. Have your hands down by your sides and about a foot in front of you, palms open toward the ground and fingers spread wide. Keep your body vertical with your head above your heart and your heart above your belly. Take a moment to appreciate the ground that is supporting you, that is under each of us. This is where understanding is found and can bring more meaning to life.

Here are some grounding questions to ask yourself.

What do I deeply care about?

What is the ground I stand on?

What qualities of being bring meaning and joy to my life?

All these questions lead to remembering who you are. Finding your ground helps you differentiate between what another is saying or doing and who you are. Take the time you need to appreciate the ground you stand on and what you deeply value.

As you gain a sense of your ground and recover your sense of self, you can move to the next step of empathizing with your partner.

5. Empathy

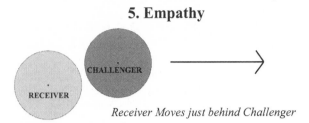

Receiver Moves just behind Challenger

This is a moment in the Spiral Blend where the lightest touch is the most powerful one. Finding what you stand on—your ground—is a necessary step to connecting to another's ground where we find understanding.

Receiver: Once you have resourced your own ground, step to just behind the shoulder of the Challenger as he continues pointing at your original position and speaking the triggering statements.

---

*In Aikido, this angle of entry is called shikaku and means "optimum entering angle."Shikaku is both a very safe position for someone to move into when attacked and the most effective angle of entry for effectively harmonizing the situation. When the Receiver steps into shikaku, centered, resourced, and ready, the dance begins between the yin and the yang, the knowing and the mystery.

Receiver: Enter with care and bring the palm of your hand directly behind the Challenger's heart, *but don't touch yet.* Just listen with an intention to connect with the Challenger's ground. Listen without agenda or pressure to "fix things." Look over the Challenger's shoulder and be open and curious to what it might be like to be in his/ her shoes. In this position, the Challenger can barely see you.

At any time, if you become too triggered or caught up in the drama of the words the Challenger is speaking, go back to the wind and ground positions to re-center.

In this moment, with heart behind heart, with your judgments and triggering out of the way, connection is nascent. There is a moment of connection that happens before touch—before the utterance of any word. As you listen to the Challenger's words, be open and wonder:

a. What is this person feeling?

b. What would this person love more of?

c. What are the deeper needs under the words?

d. What is the ground this person is standing on?

Good timing is process and patience awaiting an advantage. There is a rhythm in all communication. *There is a time to initiate and begin, a time to listen, a time for action, and a time to end.* If you don't pay attention to the space in a song and rush the beat, you hurt the song. It's the same with relationships.

The main purpose of empathic guesses is to create connection. Listen patiently and with humility. Pay attention to the rhythm of this unfolding. Give it the space it needs. Wait to be moved by a sense or some glimpse of understanding of the ground the Challenger is standing on. Only then do you make an empathic guess. Like a crescendo approaching in a song, let the urge build inside you until you feel moved. Then guess.

Receiver: To help understand the quality of presence and listening required here, try to imagine in the moment of guessing that you have traveled a great distance, climbed the mountain to be in the presence of a very wise elder, and now have an opportunity to be with such a divine individual. Imagine the qualities of humility, respect, and gratitude that would accompany your question(s).

> The name for this poignant moment in Aikido is *dai-ai*. Translated from Japanese, it means "big love." It can also be translated as "moment of engagement." It is the all-encompassing love that reminds us we are one, and our needs are one. *Dai-ai* is when you hold the other in an empathic listening field and sense the deeper intentions that are below the conflict. In Aikido, the moment of *dai-ai* happens just before any physical interaction takes place, when your own intentions are clear and you are ready so that by the time your attacker takes action, it is already over! You can literally stop the conflict before it turns physical or violent.

This is where the lightest of guesses can be the most connective. The quality of feeling behind your guess shows that you really want to understand who the other is for the sake of loving connection.

Receiver: Make sure when you speak it is clearly a question and not a statement. In time, find your own genuine way of guessing what the ground level of the other's feelings and needs is. For now, here are a couple of examples of ways to guess:

- I am guessing you feel frustrated and would love some appreciation or maybe just to be heard? Is that right?

- Are you feeling angry that I came into your room without asking because you really value privacy and want yours to be respected?

As you guess, you will know by the reaction it invokes how near or far you are from connecting with the Challenger's ground-level needs. If the guess is close, you will notice a visceral "shift" that in some way shows a release or an easing of tension as the Challenger begins to feel heard and resistance lessens.

The next beat in the rhythm of the Spiral Blend is the response from your partner. Be sure not to rush the moment between the guess and the response, or you might ruin the beauty of the song's unfolding. The heart has no need to rush. Most often it's our heads that are in a hurry. Often, your partner's response will let you know whether you are on the mark, and in some way, if you listen closely, your partner will give you breadcrumbs. Always take time to feel how your words land on your partner. If your guess was off the mark, re-center and try again. Ask a clarifying question if necessary.

When the shift does occur, savor this precious moment, and don't rush to fill the space with words. Just appreciate this quality of connection. Slow down and deeply feel it. This shift is a moment when you have moved into your heart and touched another, when the conflict becomes no longer a conflict but a place to explore collaboratively. Remember what this feels like. This creative moment is all too often rushed or missed.

Once you feel the shift and a sense of connection, gently, with the lightest of touch, place your palm on the Challenger's back. This initial touch is of the

> Another Aikido principle is called *zanshin*. It refers to a state of awareness, of relaxed alertness. The literal translation of *zanshin* is "remaining mind." It literally means being absolutely attentive to the next move right after the previous move.

utmost importance. As soon as you touch someone, they organize themselves around that touch. A compassionate touch leaves nothing to resist. In the midst of a fight, to be touched this way brings relief and intensifies the sense of connection. If the other person feels hesitancy, manipulation, or an agenda in your touch or words, a sense of mistrust can grow.

As you proceed from the last move to this one, remember all the care and effort it took to ignite the connection. Just like building a fire from scratch, once that initial, tiny flame bursts forth, the job is not done. Just the right amount of breath and kindling is needed to continue to build the fire—too much or too little and it might go out. So with your presence and attention to that small flame you have kindled, continue from when the Receiver has just put a hand on the Challenger's back.

Receiver: Open lots of space between your words and the Challenger's responses. With care and patience, continue to guess at the ground that is under the Challenger's words. Listen, and when you begin to feel resonance, like you are getting on the same page, without changing the direction, gently and slowly move the conversation forward. With your hand on the Challenger's back, gradually suggest with your touch the intention to walk for a while in the direction in which the Challenger is pointing. This movement is a suggestion, not a push.

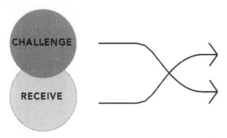

Receiver: As you feel a connection and understanding growing between the two of you, gradually move from behind the Challenger to his/her side. Continue to hold the Challenger's needs with care as you slowly and respectfully bring to the conversation what you would love and value in this moment as well. Be careful not to introduce strategies, judgments, or agendas with attachments to outcomes into the conversation. Get both of your mutual needs on the table first.

Mutual Strategies

There is a moment in Aikido practice that is called aiki. This is when conflict becomes a harmonious movement toward greater connection and understanding

Receiver: Gently, with your hand resting on the Challenger's back, continue to walk forward together. Keep your focus on the present moment and stay open to possibilities. Continue the conversation with empathy and honesty. Once you can articulate your mutual needs, mutual strategies arise easily. As mutual needs are shared, a 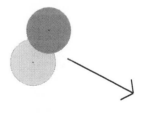 new direction is suggested. One where both Receiver and Challenger, as partners, begin to walk in a direction that honors each other's needs reflects this new collaboration.

6. Internalizing the Practice

Of course, it would look pretty silly to spread your arms and move to wind or step behind the back of the person you are speaking to in the middle of a conflict. Going through this practice with a training partner will help illuminate places where you get stuck and triggered as well as places to foster deep connection. Set up sessions to practice the Spiral Blend role-play in groups and with partners and friends. In time you will be able to move through the positions of the Spiral Blend in your mind without moving your body or by making subtle micro-movements that remind you of the full body practice. Here are some examples:

- When I want to ground, I wiggle my toes to feel the earth and imagine sending roots down.
- I turn my palms behind me to find support at my back.
- To imagine wind, I pivot my body slightly and imagine someone's words sliding off me instead of landing fully on me.

When Judith catches any of my micro-movements in the middle of our fights, she smiles because she knows the reason I am doing them is to be more present with her. Make up your own micro-movements—whatever is comfortable and will remind you of the steps in the dance.

Just as I did while jogging with my wife, find your own creative ways to mix the Spiral Blend into your daily interactions. The more you practice, the more you will glean and incorporate a way of harmonizing conflict into your being.

The Spiral Blend Stories

I led a workshop in Duncan, British Columbia, called "Finding Common Ground" that was attended by 12 fathers and their sons, ages 11 to 13. Children entering their adulthood grow and change at such a rapid pace that sometimes it's difficult for parents to make the changes within themselves that are necessary to keep up with them. A centerpiece in this training was the Spiral Blend.

In the center of the circle, John spoke to his son in a role-play that recreated a conflict they were having at home. He said: "Keep the noise down! I have to wear earplugs all day because of the noise in my carpentry shop, and I need some quiet here!" Historically, his son Andrew would nod his head and in no time make just as much noise as he'd been making before. John would invariably get angrier, and the conflict would escalate. I coached Andrew through this role-play as he stepped out of the way of his father's words and took a moment to ground himself by remembering what was most important to him. Andrew said: "I care about honesty. I care about people listening to each other well. I care about people helping one another." That's what he was willing to take a stand for in his own life. That was his ground.

He then moved to a place behind his father, looking over his dad's shoulder to imagine what his father was seeing and feeling. His heart lined up behind his dad's heart. From this position, he was able to listen to his father's raised voice without judgment or agenda. He felt centered and grounded. Andrew could now give his father some space and feel into what was underneath his words.

Connecting in that moment to his father's ground, lightly he asked, "Are you upset because you worked really hard today and need quiet to rest?" His father just stood there as Andrew added: "And maybe you'd like me to really get how hard you work to support me, too, because you care. Is that right? Am I'm getting it right, Dad?"

The room was silent. John stood there, looking stunned. His shoulders and back seemed to settle. His breath quieted. Color came to his face. His eyes became a little liquid. He just turned around, speechless, and with the gentlest appreciation said, "My son." They hugged each other. The beauty and realization of that connection rippled around the room. Empathy for one touches all. As we debriefed, John described the moment, "I felt a connection to my son that I love with my son and have so missed."

In another workshop, William was struggling with his wife Elaine. Elaine was a very intelligent, high-energy woman, a manager with a high-stress job. In a role-play, he stood behind her. He was listening to her vent about how hard it was for her to live with the chaos in their home. She said: "You throw your clothes over the chair instead of hanging them up. You always leave a dirty film in the tub that I have to clean. I am just too busy to take care of everything!"

If William had not centered prior to stepping behind her heart, he surely would have felt criticized and blamed. He still got a little uncomfortable, and his question came out a bit rushed and "heady" when he asked her, "Are you feeling angry and wanting some ease at home?"

Elaine responded, "Yes, I am angry because you never put things away."

This re-triggered William, so I asked him to go back to wind to let her words go. He grounded and remembered where he stood. He came back behind her and again listened for what was upsetting her. This time we could see that he was noticeably calmer, not taking what she was saying personally, and, with his heart behind her heart, he just listened. In almost a whisper he gently said, "Are you just needing some rest time when you come home after working all day, and want me to know that if the house was more cared for how that would really help?"

Elaine just stood there, almost stunned. It was like she was leaning on the door to get in, and all of a sudden it just opened unexpectedly. Her eyes filled with tears, her demeanor softened, and she choked out a grateful "Yes." Everyone's attention was riveted to the moment, and tears welled in several people's eyes. Connection was made.

*What we deny becomes our
destiny, what we embrace becomes
our destiny, there is a choice.*

DKW

CHAPTER ELEVEN

Working With Anger

The Power of Presence

There are scrolls that document, Aikido, written by its founder, Morhei Ueshiba, in Japanese letters/symbols called *kanji*. After his death, one core training principle that was gleaned from these scrolls was translated as "*extend ki.*" A generation later, the scrolls were reinterpreted, and this same phrase was more accurately translated as "let *ki* extend." This new translation implies a state of presence that allows more of a being than a doing. Likewise, with NVC and Somatic Consensus, a principle is to train and improve the ability to get out of our own way to *allow* empathy to occur. One friend suggested the acronym, WAIT, which stands for "why am I talking." Another friend once suggested, as a general rule, that when I feel compelled to say something, "Don't," and instead, listen and be present to whatever needs are compelling me to speak. In other words,
"Don't just say something, be there!"

I went into prison as a volunteer of the Freedom Project, a program that teaches NVC to inmates. Our weekend focus was on working with anger. I had previously trained with two members of our facilitator team and met the fourth that morning, Lucrecia, a wizened woman in her mid-80s. Immediately I felt at ease in her presence. In her thick Swiss accent, she expressed that she already felt an affinity with me and could sense that I would bring something new and special to the workshop. She engendered sincerity. During the next two days, Lucrecia spoke only once or twice a day. Her presence brought solace from the prison's harshness. At the end of the last day, one man shared how difficult

159

it was for him to express things he was feeling to his wife. He was afraid he'd do it wrong, start arguments, and be misunderstood. Lucrecia leaned toward him, clasped his hands, and said, "No matter what you do or say, if it comes from your heart, there is never any waste." Everyone in that room took it in fully.

Words convey a great deal; however, presence is where we radiate and transmit our whole being. Training our senses somatically increases the ability to listen and feel the rhythms within and around us. Over time, as training becomes more embodied, the underlying currents and cues in all interactions can become more deeply felt. Training of the heart is never wasteful. Regardless of the outcomes we think we want, life is more satisfying when we keep in mind that working in difficult relationships can sometimes be our best training.

Choice Situations

It is hard to listen well to those who trigger us most. On the positive side, anger is a catalyst to reestablish important boundaries and assert personal integrity, a sign of engagement with life and the will to live. Anger is a self-demand for things to be different. Anger is a sign that people are touched deeply by the events of their lives and feel strongly about them. Anger, like the pain of a cut, tells us to pay attention and tend to the situation.

Anger is valuable as an alarm clock that wakes us up to present needs that are not being met, while acting out of anger habitually creates a heavy-handedness in which our actual needs are unlikely to be met. Anger becomes a problem when it becomes habitual, because as an emotion it has limitations and uses a great deal of energy without providing much direct benefit. Used as a wake-up call, anger can point toward a source of healing.

Whenever we are confronted with someone's behavior that stimulates our own anger, a choice situation arises. Anger results when we choose the option of finding fault and blaming others for our own intense feelings. Anger then becomes a game where we think another is deserving of punishment as we sit in judgment of their "wrongness." Faultfinding and blaming others, whether conscious or not, exacerbates feelings of anger. It is a movement backward. It does not address the underlying needs, so the conflict heats up even more. Conflict is like someone trying to tell us something important. If we ignore them, they more often than not get louder. If ignored, anger can turn to violence. Anger that is fixated on or overindulged masks the source of the pain that the anger is there to reveal in the first place. Learn to tolerate and appreciate the intense feelings of anger, catch the feeling, discover the needs, the source of the anger, and then breathe. Catch and release.

Stop Taking Others Personally

Anger felt is something stimulated—but never caused—by other people's behavior. Sometimes this is really hard to swallow, especially in times of intense pain. But hey, aren't there times when anger is justified or righteous? What about in the face of a corporation that pollutes a river that you love, child abuse, abandonment, or a painful divorce? We want to find reasons for our pain. In truth, all anger is stimulated by life-alienating, violent, provocative thinking. I believe the enemy images we cultivate and project mask the truth of our humanity, and to whatever degree we blame others for what we feel, we also contribute to the violence on this planet.

As a volunteer for the Freedom Project, I've heard story after story from inmates about the violence they've perpetrated on others because they've framed others as the reason for their own violent acts. One day, as I stepped into a circle to greet the inmates in one of my trainings, there was something about one of the men that gave me the creeps, so I gave him a wide berth. Over the weekend as we listened, he shared his pain, his vulnerability, and his desire for a better life. My "enemy" image of him faded, and what emerged was our shared struggle to become less violent and more loving.

This work in prison opened me to places I imprison and hide in myself. As a society, we've disassociated ourselves from millions of incarcerated fellow humans who we would rather label as bad and forget. Consider, for a moment, how it would be if we re-framed inmates as people who hold a key to understanding our own wholeness as individuals and as a society. It will be a great day when we can re-create prison as a place of healing instead of punishment, where each inmate can come to see his or her own humanity through the lenses of heartfelt listening.

Anger expressed when connected to its roots is powerful and moving. Anger can also co-opt our energy if the focus is to punish rather than tending to the cause of the anger (unmet needs). Angry feelings are our own responsibility to tend to instead of tricking ourselves into believing another is the cause. Let's look at anger and punishment somatically.

Anger

- What is the first thing I want to remember when I become angry?

- How do I know when I am angry, and what would help me notice it sooner?

- Are there any patterns to my anger (body sensation, words, strategies, etc.)?

- What are my recurrent triggers, unmet needs, and feelings?

Punishment

- Fill in the blank: "I don't like people who ...."

- Notice how it feels in your body to make a punitive judgment.

- Now re-frame your thinking to take responsibility for your anger, such as: "When people do... I feel anxious."

- Notice the difference.

Stop Taking Others Personally

S.S.S.T.O.P. is a simple practice we teach in prison to turn anger into resources for connection.

1. Sensations: When you become angry, notice any physical sensations in your body: tightness, tingling, discomfort, heaviness.

2. Stimulus: Observe what actually happened factually. What did you hear, see, and smell that was the stimulus for your anger. Observe with as little judging or evaluating of what you see as possible. Describe what you see as something you have caught on a video camera.

3. Should thinking: Feel and discern in the present moment any judgments, labels, blame, what you think people should or should not do, be, or deserve. Notice any should thoughts that come up for you. "They should..." or "I should..."

4. Translate should thoughts to needs: Listen for the unfulfilled needs underneath your should thinking. Get in touch with what you truly need. Breathe and feel. When I make this judgment, what am I needing and not getting? What is it that I would love that is missing here and now?

5. Open to feelings: Tolerate, relax, and open into your anger and what it is telling you that you deeply need. Be open to the emotions that are underneath: e.g. feelings of despair, sorrow, hurt, fear, shame...

6. Present request: Make a doable request to yourself and/or the other person using concrete, positive language that addresses the source of the anger.

Whenever we perceive someone as an adversary, regardless of the words we speak, our presence transmits the judgments we carry and what we truly feel.

On some level, we are not fooling anyone when we try to hide our intentions and feelings. We've all experienced times when our carefully chosen words leave our listener(s) feeling upset or confused. Others sense and mistrust when our words and feelings do not align. Words can free our thinking or imprison our souls. The words we say are only the tip of the iceberg compared to the messages we project through body language, voice tone, gestures, facial expression, and other non-verbal cues. Language patterns reinforce cultural imperatives, which may or may not be helpful. Used over and over, speech patterns become deeply embedded and are challenging to change because they exist beneath our radars in daily interactions.

Re-framing: Changing the Channel

My next-door neighbor, John, was a dedicated pack-rat. Strong willed, independent, somewhat cantankerous, he was always on the look out for discarded materials and recycled things which he accumulated into a huge pile at the end of his driveway. This pile was just out of view of his house and in plain sight of mine! It was the first thing I saw as I approached my home and the last thing I viewed upon leaving. Over the years, much of it weathered and became unusable and unsightly garbage. My requests for him to move the pile were met with negative reactions. The pile only grew. I am embarrassed to say how angry this made me. After 15 years of this, right before he moved away, he revealed that, in part, he had kept the pile because he knew how much it bugged me.

If we don't face our anger, we are controlled by it. One effective strategy for moving from relational sand traps into more positive places is the practice of "re-framing." An example of re-framing might look like this: A person has missed an appointment with you. If you frame this person as lazy or uncaring, you may feel angry. If you re-frame this person as someone who is confused and in deep pain, you may feel more compassion and patience. Another example: Your child is screaming in the middle of a store. If you frame this child as unruly and belligerent, you may be moved to anger and punitive strategies. If you re- frame and see the child's screaming as an expression of confusion and the need for attention, you most likely will be called to other ways of handling the situation.

Re-framing changes the channel when we get stuck in our thinking and need a fresh perspective. With John, my re-framing was to see him as my "Lucifer." Lucifer is commonly thought of as the Devil, something to avoid at all costs. But Lucifer was actually an angel, and the name means "Light Bringer." In my re-frame, my reactions to John's ways of being shone a light on places inside me that would otherwise never see the light of day. In my martial arts training, the best training partners keep me on my toes. They are those who are the most unpredictable and challenging. I re-framed John as a good training partner. My relationship to John helped uncover places in me that needed attention and healing and that I might never have seen on my own within more comfortable relationships.

I was not the only one who struggled with John. We had many community meetings in which John raised his lone blocking concerns that mired our consensus process for endless meetings. Making decisions was often difficult together. There was plenty of contention; however, through it we gained skills for navigating our differences more honorably. It took a while to accept the principle that the work of learning to understand and value one another is itself an accomplishment and that getting to know one another in this way is at least as important (maybe more so) as whatever project we were working on.

Over the years, endeavoring to listen empathically and speak in more compassionate ways facilitated more amicable relationships. Valuing connection first and strategies second produced the most generative outcomes. John never did clean up his pile. He made a few attempts, but it did not seem to be in his nature. Much of who he is remains a mystery to me. At the same time, I am forever grateful for certain moments of connection we had and a relationship that gave me opportunities to learn how to work with my anger and to find patience and understanding in ways that continue to serve me well in all my relationships.

Here is a partner practice to explore re-framing somatically:

Test 1:

Person A: Make a fist and extend your arm straight out in front of you at a 90 degree angle from your body. Hold your arm stiffly as strongly as you can and say, "I hate war."

Person B: In an even, non-jerking motion, put your hand on Person A's fist and push down. Notice how much strength it takes to push it down. Person A: Notice how much strength it takes to resist.

Test 2:

Person A: Again make a fist and extend your arm straight out in front of you at a 90 degree angle from your body, but this time Person A says with feeling, "I love peace."

Person B: In an even, non-jerking motion, push down on Person A's fist.

Both people notice the difference in the amount of pressure needed between loving peace and hating war.

Loving peace and hating war are two very different frames of reference and produce very different somatic experiences. Peace describes a time when our attention is focused on what we are drawn to, on what interests us, on what we want. War describes a state where we fight against what we do not want. Our energies go to opposing that which we fear and attacking and defending rather than to creating. How we frame our perceptions affects where our mind goes, affects our energy, motivation, and enthusiasm. Becoming aware, sharing and changing the frameworks that exist in each of us, makes more space for new and inclusive strategies to emerge that support inter-group, inter-human, and in-ter-species consciousness.

A HEAVEN/EARTH PRACTICE

Here is a movement and visualizing practice for relaxing and settling your system when anger arises. It is distilled from Aikido practice and takes only a few minutes. Remember, the more relaxed you are, the more aware you can be, and the better you can utilize your deeper understanding and your higher knowing.

Heaven/Earth

1. Begin standing with head above heart above belly. Soften your eyes and take a deep relaxing breath.

2. Bend from the knees and touch the earth with a sense of gratitude for how it supports you.

3. As you come to standing, reach straight out to the sides, palms up, and slowly bring your arms up in a wide arch. As you do so, take in a deep breath and imagine all of the resources and relationships that are available around you. Your palms meet directly above your head. Bring your palms together so that your fingers are pointing toward the sky, and look up.

4. As you reach for the sky, imagine gathering what it is that gives your life joy and brings lightness to your being, your highest values. Appreciate this as you bring your hands and these resources down toward your belly center.

5. When your hands are in front of your belly, point your fingers toward the ground and start the whole exercise again. Repeat three or more times.

Mind in the Belly

1. The third time your hands come to your belly, put your left hand over your right hand, and cup your hands together so the fingers on your left hand point toward the earth, and on your right hand toward the sky. This is kind of a three-dimensional yin/yang shape. Leave enough space between the palms for a small egg to fit in. Put these clasped hands right on your belly, just under your belly button, making sure there is physical connection to your belly and no gap between your body and hands.

2. Now shake your cupped hands vigorously up and down so that your belly shakes as well. This hand shaking motion is an Aikido practice called *Fute Tamashi*. It is a Japanese phrase that in English means, "soul shaking." It helps us connect and open up to our belly center, the hara. In Aikido practice, the *hara* is where physical and spiritual power originate.

"A pure mind coming from a pure heart brings joy that can fill the whole space between heaven and earth." Rick Haltermann, Curriculum of the Soul

Our Sixth and Seventh Senses

Re-framing helps us become aware of and process anger, arrogance, and other negative emotions that hinder us from seeing clearly what is happening around us. The creative energy that is key to progress cannot be accessed with a negative attitude. Anger obscures our sixth and seventh senses.

- The sixth sense is intuition that comes through empathy, which can sense the intent and imminent moves of another. The sixth sense incorporates all the information gathered through our physical senses and connects us empathically to our higher consciousness.

- The seventh sense is the wisdom that allows us to learn from and maintain an awareness of the laws of nature. The seventh sense is our sense that connects patterns of nature with the patterns and purposes of our practices.

We can quietly watch an ocean wave to learn the lessons of power and efficiency in its movements. It is our seventh sense that guides the appreciation that to harm another is to harm oneself and to see us all as one rather than a patchwork of individual parts at war. Master Aikidoist, Mitsugi Saotome, described it like this: "When you listen to music, you do not listen to it note by note. To understand its beauty, it must be listened to as a whole. The seventh sense is the ability to hear the whole music of the life in which you participate and to hear how the note you sound fits into the song of which you are a part." Noticing the analogies between patterns in nature and those we sense in our bodies helps us understand our own life and create effective ecological strategies.

It is possible that the next Buddha will not take the form of an individual. The next Buddha may take the form of a community—a community practicing understanding and loving kindness, a community practicing mind full living. This may be the most important thing we can do for the earth.

Thich Nhat Hanh

CHAPTER TWELVE

The Ecology of Relationship

The Real Web

As members of the US consumer class in this age of technology and global communication, we experience a degree of personal independence like no other time in history. The price we've paid is a decline in the kind of relationships and communities that feed our deep need for belonging and the increased damage to the commons we all share. Imagine for a moment that every interaction with another person creates a thread between you that connects you. After decades of daily and varied experiences, these threads proliferate and become a fabric that intensifies the connection and understanding, much like what is found within the bonds of a healthy family. Now imagine that quality of care and collaboration rippling outward to other households, the greater community, and the environment. In time, this web becomes dense and empathic to create a tactile sense of place. These threads, felt, connect us to the soil, rocks, plants, water, weather, other humans, and the animal world. We can listen to the chords of the strings of this instrument, strummed by deep remembrance. Home is a cave, a burrow, a tree, a cottage, a nest, a river, a room, an ocean, a hilltop. Community is the invisible strings we hear singing. Community is the blueprint of life and the web of meaning we spin around each other. It is a fact of life and the context in which all life and everything human takes place. Birds gather in flocks, whales swim in pods, buffalo travel in herds, and for the vast majority of human existence, our ancestors lived in tribes. It is essential that our modern societies not forsake the wisdom that evolved over countless millennia. Although I am not advocating that we should all go back to tribal life, we must humble ourselves enough to begin to see what it is that we have forsaken and cannot fully understand in order to reclaim what we need to flourish.

The modern propensity for human beings to foul our own nest is an indicator of just how disconnected from our embodied wisdom, our somas, we have become. From species that we have yet to meet being wiped out daily, to armed children in genocidal wars, the consequences of our choices are apparent. The thought of passing on a diminished world to our children, suffering instead of wisdom, must awaken us to take a stand for what is worth caring about. Our choice is not whether we want to make a difference, but how, and then to take one step at a time.

Practice of Community

Community is a daily practice. The practices in this book are centered on embodying the skills and presence for generating community wherever we are. Community cultivates our own self-respect, respect for others, and ultimately respect for all of life. It is within the fullness of community that we are challenged and guided to become more open and compassionate, to listen better, to explore beyond ourselves and be responsible to our connections. In human relationships, there are many kinds of community. The basics found in the tapestry of community are cultivated wherever our lives weave through seasons of celebrations, struggles, births, and deaths. The fabric reflects daily life: traumas, meetings, playing, arguing, working together, taking steps, building structures, gardening, separation, falling down, raising children, family conflicts, forgiveness, young ones becoming teens, sharing meals, marriage, and elderhood.

In the formative years of our intentional community, developing bylaws and guidelines, working with the county, developing our common spaces, putting in roads, gardens, and utilities as most of us raised young children and held down jobs was profoundly challenging. Familial and cultural patterns of hierarchy, sexism, classism, adultism, ageism, racism, ignorance, and the fears that sponsor them played themselves out in our small circle of well-intentioned people. When triggered by conflict, we do not rise to our higher ideals; we fall back to what we have practiced most in our lives—behaviors born out of the family and culture that nurtured us. Things felt like a pressure cooker of relationships in a house of mirrors that relentlessly reflected back to us our own selves as things unfolded. Our struggles took us far beyond our comfort zones but clarified, at the very least, what we did not know. They also provided ample motivation to find more inclusive, forgiving, and responsible ways to be together. Our community now encompasses four generations, and it becomes clearer, as we continually break new ground, that we've only scratched the surface of the potential. It is not an easy road, *and* you will not find a greater advocate for this type of adventure than I am!

Glimpses

Early on, we found precious few elders we could ask for guidance—who had experience growing up in an intact, healthy community—or even a family in which intergenerational relationships were still a part of daily life. As decades go by, we are growing our own elders who can pass on experiences of multi-genera-tional living. Along the way, we get glimpses of what a healthy, mature community can offer, and this continues to galvanize our efforts.

At a recent birth in our community, everyone gathered to help where they could—making food, watching children, readying the home, and assisting with whatever was needed to welcome the newborn child. This child was literally sung into the world and landed in a welcoming circle of community the moment she was birthed. Seeing how the children flourish are the signs that we are heading in a good direction.

Months earlier, an elder member died. During his last 10 years, his Alzheimer's disease progressed, and he grew more and more forgetful. He was at all our dinners and gatherings. He had a place in our community. On occasion, the clouds of forgetfulness cleared, and he recited a favorite poem or sang an old song he loved. On the night of his death, his family and many of us in the community, young and old, gathered around him and read those poems to him. He passed as we sang him one of his favorite songs.

I cannot imagine a more beautiful way for a child to be brought into the world or an elder to leave. I've known most of the children in my community since they were born. Some of those children are now grown, and their children are a part of my daily life. The community has its own life that everyone—young and old—feed. Death and birth, the cycles of life, like the changes of season, shared and experienced in common, bring a quality of life that touches a deep yearning for community, where everyone is counted as belonging.

Reclaiming Community

Reclaiming community is similar to reclaiming a forest that has been clear-cut. First we plant trees in rows. They grow and eventually provide a canopy and compost for new growth to flourish below. Younger trees and undergrowth sprout up. Diversity occurs and invites more. Over time, animals, plants, and organisms self-select. Some thrive and flourish, while others leave or die off. In time, a more robust, integrated, inter-dependent system evolves out of the original mono-culture. Organisms develop more and more symbiotically as countless subtle connections form a collective wholeness. Walking in an ancient forest or somewhere in the heart of the remaining places where Mother Nature is whole and unadulterated, the collective life of this planet is most potently felt. What affects one directly, affects all indirectly. Gracefully making the always necessary and the forever-unfinished corrections *to shift between what you need and our mutual needs* is key.

Over the decades, like the symbiotic relationships of an aging forest, something organic and far bigger than its parts is developing in my community and in me. What's emerging is a visceral experience of community as a way of being that is transmitted from within each of us—a dynamic, evolving process through which the world and self can be effectively transformed. The practice of community is to continuously learn over time better ways to get back up more gracefully after we fall, to honor and add diversity to the mix, and to more and more clearly recognize that we are all in this together. There are no illusions. My community has divorces, violent moments, schisms, and pain. That is all part of life. Community, however we cultivate it, offers context, meaning, and a ground to stand on in this whirlpool of life. In my community, our original vision continues to become a reality in ways we could never have imagined when we began. We are learning how to "conflict well," and from that "well," we all drink deeply.

The world desperately needs ways to live that acknowledge human differences in just this way. Cultural diversity is essential for a healthy human ecosystem. A theme of honor and gratitude weaves through vital communities, and just as there are many stages of life, there is always more to learn about what community truly is. At its most basic levels, community life reminds us daily of our direction and purpose, renews our self-regard, and affirms that connection is possible. I believe a renaissance of community spirit, based in relatedness and wholeness, is necessary if we are to have a healthy world for our children to grow up in.

READING QUALITIES

Every word on the needs list in NVC (Appendix B) is a quality of being. Each quality is expansive, and when fully explored, connects with the others. They are each facets of the same gem, of our wholeness. We are always transmitting the qualities of our emotional states of being. The qualities felt by others through our presence determine the quality of connection we manifest. If words and actions do not align with the felt qualities of our presence and intention, a double message is transmitted. Learning to discern and attune to the underlying qualities we send in our interactions helps simplify our choices, offers direction, and cultivates connection.

In uncertain moments, to find clarity and inner guidance, we can ask ourselves: "Is what I am saying coming from love and care?" "What would integrity do at this point?" "Are my strategies coming from a place of insecurity?" "Is my heart into this?"

This is a partner practice for empathically reading and speaking one another's qualities and virtues. Trust is fundamental to the harmony of a relationship. Honor and respect is a direct route to trust. A powerful way to respect another is to be able to notice and at times speak their virtuous qualities, publicly and privately. Virtuous qualities are the result of putting your values into action. Each individual has a core of underlying values that contribute to his or her system of beliefs, ideas, or opinions. Though we all have values, applying them with integrity can be a difficult task. Societies have values that are shared among many of the participants in that culture. There are qualities that come naturally to us, and others that come less easily. For example, a virtue of my son Devin that I notice is how upright he is. His integrity is felt. That is something that he seems to have been born with. I also notice that he does not seek the limelight, and yet he has made choices in his life that naturally put him in leadership positions in groups he's involved with. Devin has cultivated virtues of leadership, of speaking his mind with care and dignity. Leading does not seem to be his first nature. It is something he has worked to develop in order to contribute his gifts to the world.

Focusing on virtues and values not only allows us to act in a better way, it also allows us to react in a way that is true to our own value systems. Often we may find that our thoughts become clouded when we are thrust into the chaos of everyday life. Speaking our virtues builds a generosity of spirit in our body. The more grounded and specific we are, the more powerful we are. Practice being kind. Be virtuous. Build trust. Align with your values. Train in joy.

Set Up

1. Sit or stand facing one another. Settle yourselves with a deep breath. Take turns. The first person asks permission to share the qualities that he or she is about to share. The permission that our family, partners, friends, and associates grant us to speak honestly and directly about them is sacred. When others are open to how we listen to them, they are honoring the shared commitment to the relationship. To then speak our own hearts is to respect this openness.

2. Ask your partner: "Would you like it if I spoke your virtues?"

3. For each of the following practices, one person speaks as the other listens. Take 1-2 minutes per turn. Let the words spoken settle in. Give ample space to appreciate what was said, then switch roles.

4. Pause, and then move to the next practice. Give plenty of space in between each practice. Remember to speak both the qualities that you sense come

easily and the ones that come with work over time.

Practice

1. Speak your practice partner's virtuous qualities.
2. Speak the virtuous qualities of another in the room.
3. Speak the virtuous qualities of your intimate partner or a family member.
4. Speak the virtuous qualities of a teacher in your life.
5. Speak your own virtuous qualities. Tell your partner.

Resources at Our Backs

We live in a society where the individual is often glorified at the expense of the collective. Consequently, many of us exhaust ourselves by thinking we are alone and will not get the help we need because it does not occur to us to ask for it. We lose sight of the people and resources that are readily available. In this regard, there is much healing work to do. We cannot be whole alone because healing is impossible in loneliness.

Over the years, working in many cultures around the world, I have asked people to bring their attention to what is at their back. I ask them: "Who's got your back? What kind of support from others do you feel back there? Do you feel like you have support, or do you mostly think you have to do it all by yourself?" For some, these are unfamiliar, often startling questions. Why? Because most of us have *practiced* a belief that we must go it alone, we are startled by another possibility. Everywhere in our language you can see the imagery and qualities our backs represent in phrases such as "he has no backbone," "talking behind your back," "I've got your back," "back down," "don't get your back up," "he has no one to back him up." Our backs ache when we think we must carry the weight of our lives alone. In truth, we are a part of something bigger. We have more-resources than we can imagine.

When I sit in a sweat lodge with my Native American friends, we call in all our ancestors with gratitude to seek guidance. During a Passover Seder from my Jewish heritage's tribal roots, I eat the food of my ancestors to remember their passage from slavery to freedom, their struggles, and their virtues. Indigenous cultures around the world listen to the wisdom of those who came before them, the ancestors at their backs. In Western culture, our focus—habitually and metaphorically—goes to what is in *front* of us, what we are doing, where we are going, and what needs to get done. Rarely do we consciously bring our attention to what is at our back, to our histories, to what can support us from behind and the healing that is possible by doing so.

RESOURCES AT OUR BACKS

This simple and elegant practice accesses the qualities, wisdom, and support of those who came before us. Here we can utilize NVC practices to connect with those around us who might not be available or still alive. This requires us to muster our imaginations. By doing so, with time and practice, we can explore the qualities and virtues that we would love to have more of in our own lives at any given moment.

1. Choose Your Helpers

Stand with your head above your heart and your heart above your belly in a vertical line. With your hands by your sides and about 12 inches from your torso, turn your palms to the space behind you. Like radar dishes that pick up signals, imagine feeling the space behind you. It is a common thing in my trainings for some participants to have difficulty imagining the support behind them. A common story and practice is, "I have to do it all on my own, and there is no one to support me but me." When this is the story and experience, all the focus becomes about what is happening in front of us, and we lose sight of what is behind.

If you are finding it difficult or unfamiliar to bring your attention behind you, ask friends to put a hand on your back, then let your attention surround them, or lean with your back against the wall to feel the reality of something behind you. You can also imagine a large, soft cushion that supports your whole backside.

Imagine and choose a person who has come before you who embodies a quality or virtue you would love to have a little more of in your own life. This might be an elder relative, an ancestor who is no longer alive, a teacher, or a great teacher in the world (past or present), or simply someone who has positively affected you in a way that you love. Pick just one.

*If you pick an ancestor, make sure you choose one who was healthy and whole. Be discerning. Imagining the realness of this process, you want to be mindful and respectful of what you truly wish to cultivate.

2. Remember

Remember *one* quality this person has (had) that moved you. Remember how it feels to be in the presence of this virtue. Some examples of this might be the expressiveness of Martin Luther King, the humility of Nelson Mandela, the devotion of Mother Teresa, the tenderness of your next-door neighbor, or your father's dignity.

In this "field" behind you, visualize the person whose qualities you admire placing a hand gently on your back. Feel this support. Pick just one of the qualities of this person that you would love to experience more of in yourself. Imagine the beauty of the quality of this person behind you. Since you are mostly space, you are porous. The resources behind you can come through you.

3. Write

To develop a sense of the quality, it helps to write a colorful, creative description about the person you chose. Vividly describe this person so you can literally feel what you truly love about them. In your writing, explore how their presence has touched you. Write as much or as little as you want. Most important, let your writing inspire a whole-body impression and feeling of the quality you love about this person. In this way, you can cultivate a somatic impression that you can remember and more readily draw up as needed. The more you can enliven your imagination, the more resources become available. Here is a personal example of an old friend of mine that I now bring through me:

> As a young man, I left college to apprentice as a goldsmith at a very fine, four-generation jewelry firm in Detroit. I supplemented my apprentice wages with evening jobs and lived in a very tough neighborhood. Working day and evening, I had very little social life. When I met John Hazlett, I was 22, and he was 63. John and I literally worked back-to-back for three years. There were two elderly goldsmiths at the shop. The other goldsmith, Ted, was a very fine goldsmith. He guarded his trade secrets. John, on the other hand, called me over whenever he was working on something interesting. He had a gentle smile with a touch of wryness and a genuine humility that made me immediately feel welcome. He loved to make me smile when I was upset or feeling sad, and he'd always find a way to make me laugh.

> To this day, I can feel his grandfatherly love as I rested my chin on his shoulder and watched his masterful hands setting a gemstone or shaping a ring. He showed me anything I wanted to learn. No secrets. I never heard him utter an angry word to anyone. I miss him dearly and am ever grateful for his presence in my life.

John died many years ago, but a deep impression of his kindness remains. I recall his image, his words, his mannerisms, his way of making me laugh, and his virtues. I feel him at my back. As I let this come through me, invariably a smile comes to my face, my breathing becomes more rhythmic, and my chest and shoulders relax. Moving from this "shape" and intention of kindness draws more of it into my life. Like attracts like. Instead of trying to think of what kindness feels like, I can pull from what is at my back to call up exactly what I need...always accessible...always there.

4. Apply

Maybe you don't know what to say to that challenging, triggering person who is confronting you, but there is most assuredly someone behind you who does! Maybe it is your Aunt Judith; maybe it is Gandhi. Maybe you don't have what it takes to deal with a certain person. There are many resources at your back that can come through you if you choose to connect to your support. In times of conflict, here is a practice you can do alone or explore in a role-play for bringing the resources at your back through you:

1. Imagine a triggering moment you have had with someone in your life. Set up the role-play to recreate a triggering scenario. For starters, let the triggering moment be no more than a 2 on a scale of 1 to 10. Otherwise it may become a little difficult to learn the basics of this practice.

2. As the person in front of you speaks, allow yourself to be triggered, and then respond without censoring yourself. Take notice of what you say and how you say it.

3. Begin again, and this time, before you respond, feel into and connect with who is now at your back and the qualities you admire in them and would love a bit more of in this moment.

4. Slowly imagine that quality from behind coming into and then through you. As the feeling of the quality moves through you, continue to keep it flowing by remembering to keep the connection at your back. Become it.

5. Let the urge to speak originate from your back and be the source of your words. Now, within that same mildly triggering moment, say what comes naturally to you and notice how you feel and what is different.

*Keep in mind that in this process of reconnecting with the support at your back, you may feel a sense of sweet sorrow. The sadness is grief for the love and support that you have missed for so long, and the sweetness is the celebration of reconnection with it once again, much like the experience of reuniting with an old and missed dear friend. (See Chapter 6 Two Sides of Gratitude for more on this).

Intuitive Impressions

Many people have asked me what suggestions I have for how to choose people to live with when starting an intentional community. Here is some hard won advice. First, the people in my community were not all friends before we started.

I knew some people, a few I had never met, some people were close friends, and some of us joined in spite of a lack of chemistry with another. If you are looking to find people to build a community, here are five criteria I have found useful in selecting and vetting members:

1. Trust your first intuitive impressions. You may be living with these people for a very long time. Pay attention to these initial reads and be careful not to think them away. We pick up so much information about others below and before our rational thoughts and judgments kick in. Over time, I've come to realize how spot on my initial intuitive reads are.

2. Make sure those you consider have a well-developed "generosity muscle." As you get to know each other, see if they lean more toward taking or giving. If you find someone with an attitude of "How can I help?" that is a great start. Invite them over and see what they bring. Notice if they ask how they can help, if they help clear the table, or better yet, if they offer to help wash the dishes after the gift of a meal.

3. Make sure they like to get their back into what they do. If you have a garden, invite them over to help one day, and watch if they dig into it. Have a work party for some good cause, and watch how they participate. Notice if their participation feels fully from their core, or more partial. A general rule is that if someone can get their back into their physical work, that translates to emotional work as well. Living in community takes constant emotional work.

4. Look for humility. If someone who wants to join truly believes they understand community and knows just what it takes, and therefore their opinions are very important, beware! The people in my community who thought they knew the most coming in were the most difficult people to work with, and they did not last. Look for people who are open to new ways, curious, excited to learn about what they don't know. Probably the greatest asset for flourishing in community is the wisdom and curiosity to walk into its mystery with a beginner's mind so you can receive its gifts.

5. To gain more perspective, try different settings with the people you are interested in. Watch how they work with other individuals and how they navigate groups. Some people are very comfortable one on one, but in groups, they become overwhelmed or dominant. When we become overwhelmed, idiosyncrasies and habits of behavior come more to the forefront and become visible. Take note of the default modes of people you are considering living with; it will inform you what you might be in for.

6. Find others who appreciate and can hold paradox well. People with a visceral clarity who recognize that we cannot know "me" without appreciating "we" and visa versa are less prone to side-taking strategies and more likely to embrace the fact that we are all in this together.

The body never lies.

Martha Graham

—

The body repeats the landscape.
They are the source of each other and create each other.

Meridel Le Sueur

—

We abuse the land because we regard it as a commodity belonging to
us.
When we see land as a community to which we
belong, we may begin to use it with love and
respect.

Aldo Leopold

The Missing Ingredient

A Recipe for Community

By Judith Weinstock

Our personal health and the health of the planet are bosom buddies. They suckle from the same teat. The need for sustenance connects us to all life, and as such, our role as stewards of the land and the strategies we employ to answer to our hunger is pivotal in the health of planet.

Empathy is born with the beating of our hearts and becomes fully engaged when we are placed at the breast and begin to nurse. From that moment on, our very muscles develop around the primal experience of being fed and loved to provide a sense of belonging and wellbeing.

Feeding is primal for all species. In human life, this act can be the ultimate and generative multi-tasking in the building and honoring of community in the most beautiful and profound ways. When we gather around the fire or table to eat, we have already engaged in relationship to the community of life that we find on our plate; at the same time, we are feeding the community of life that is our body, a magical internal ecosystem; and lastly, in the sharing of the meal we are nurturing and honoring the community that sits at the table with us to nurture our sense of belonging and wellbeing.

Cultural food traditions invite us to the table to taste, smell, touch, see and hear the story of a people and a place, and the intimacy between the two forged by mutual benefit over time. These traditions inform the body collective to confirm our belonging to a community, the foundation that develops our seventh sense. This "seventh sense" is described by Master Aikidoist Mitsugi Saotome as "…..the ability to hear the whole music of the life in which you participate and to hear how the note you sound fits into the song of which you are a part." The power of food traditions to develop, protect and reflect the bond between a people and a place is revealed in a quote I recently read by an anonymous Vietnamese person that said, "…after thirty years of war and occupation, our dietary customs are the only tangible signs that we still exist as a people."

In these modern times, particularly in Western culture, we have lost a *knowing of belonging to* a people and a place through time. In this disconnection, *all communities suffer*: human communities, all other species that commune through the food chain, and the earth, air and water that make it all possible.

How do we create conditions to begin the journey back to our "seventh sense"? How do we generate community?

I believe it is possible simply by focusing our attention inward. We must come home to our bodies, this *being* that has a wisdom all its own. All the poking, prodding, dissecting and diagnosing of our bodies that we humans do brings us some enlightenment, although more often than not these illuminations simply confirm the magical mystery tour that we are gifted at birth to embark on. We can reclaim community because, *gratefully*, we have our bodies, the first community we are born into. We have, in our very hearts and hands, the ingredients needed to reclaim and recalibrate our empathic faculties. We viscerally experience our first "communion" at birth, which becomes the imprint to recognize community from that moment on. Our bodies are the source, the archive of our entire histories wherein our feelings and needs reside. As such, we can tenderly visit and listen to them without judgment or shame. We can ask questions of our bodies that have no right or wrong answers, communicating trust that any answer is precisely the information we are seeking.

In these practices we are invited to participate in the intimacy of how "…the note you sound fits into the song of which you are a part". In the process we can celebrate our part in returning health and wellbeing for all life. For, within a global food system in a global economy, this most personal human act has taken on profound public ramifications like no other time in history. This is fortunate; three times a day it is in our power to bring peace and harmony back to the world!

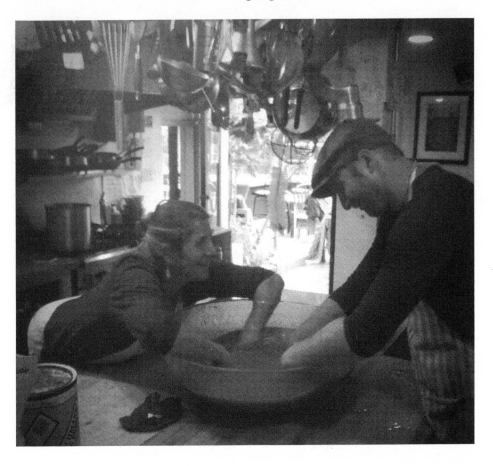

SOMATIC FOOD PRACTICES

The following is a series of inquiries to cross-train, for the purpose of integrating feelings (where they are located), thoughts (cognitive understanding), what we deeply care about (needs consciousness) and *gut* (intuition): *head, above heart, above belly*. I find it helpful to consider them an exploration without attachment to outcome, to communicate to our bodies that we are present and listening to whatever wisdom presents itself.

For this purpose I have found it helpful to keep a journal nearby to jot down gleanings that resonate in a way that you might want to come back to later for further investigation.

To Begin:

Sit vertically upright, *head, above heart, above belly*. Take a deep, relaxing breath, emitting an open-mouth releasing sound when exhaling. Ask the following questions to your body. Ask each question with a quality of curiosity and active listening. Also, invite your senses and imagination to listen for answers that you might not otherwise hear.

Notice the stimulus:

My watch says noon. Lunch time!
My friend asked me out for lunch.
I'm feeling light headed.
My stomach is growling.
My mother just called and told me she was coming to visit.
.....*what is the most common stimulus that causes you to
begin thinking about eating?*

Identify the Feeling:

Am I hungry?
How do I know I am hungry?
Where do I locate the sensations in my body that tell me this?

Be specific. Notice and acknowledge, with the lightest of your attention, any feelings that are not actually physical feelings of hunger, such as boredom, nervousness, anxiety, fear, anger or excitement. *I find it helpful to jot these down in my journal for my own later learning.*

What is my first response to those "feelings" in my body that are telling me I am hungry?

> Do I ignore it?
> Grab the first food in sight?
> Think about what I would like to eat?
> Think about what I think I *should* eat?
> Get in the car and drive up to a fast food window?
> Go for a run and wait it out?
> Make myself a beautiful meal and invite a friend over?
> Something else......?

Identify Your Needs

What do I care about and value most when feeding myself?

(The need for sustenance, primal as it is, presents a crossroads of multiple investigations to support our strategic choices for answering to our hunger. This section supports cross-training for identifying and integrating what we deeply value to inform these strategies to ensure alignment with the vision of the world we wish to participate in).

Sustenance?	Love?	Ease?
Connection?	Empathy?	Responsibility?
Excitement?	Play?	Beauty?
Generosity?	Creativity?	
Mutuality?	Integrity?	

Choose Your (new) Strategies. More Questions To The Body:

After identifying your stimulus, feelings, responses and needs, choose your strategy(ies) from a place of intention and clarity. I find that I often have multiple needs that inform how I am going to go about feeding myself. For instance, connection is foundational for me on multiple levels: connecting to what my body is asking for comes first; next comes connecting to the earth as I gather ingredients; then connecting to loved ones if I am sharing a meal. Being responsible to the earth that supports my life is important to me, so I make sure I gather as many local ingredients as possible, and if not local, then I look for ingredients that are labeled Fair Trade. I harvest and compost mindfully. Creativity, Play and Beauty are important to me, so I have fun visioning how I am going to cut something, shape something, platter something, and have it look beautiful on the plate—a feast for the eyes to tease my tongue!!!

Bringing Joy To The Table—further conversations and details of delight!
....*ask your body:*

What would sustain me perfectly right now?" (Be as specific as possible):

- Sweet?

- Sour?

- Starchy?

- Bitter?

- Soupy? Chunky? Smooth?

- Purple? Orange? White? Pink? Red?

- Soft? Hard? Crunchy? Silky?

- Cold? Hot? Cold and hot together?

- Cooked? Raw? Cooked and raw together?

Actively engage in each act of preparing your meal. This process is love and gratitude in action! In this vein, more questions you might ask yourself are:

- *When I cut this carrot, what shape would be most pleasing to my eye and my tongue?*

- *How would this meal give me pleasure to look at on my plate, or in my bowl?*

- *Would I like to eat alone or with somebody?*

- *Would I like music or silence?*

- *Would I like to sit at a table, on the couch, or on the floor?*

Taking the time to listen to our bodies is love in action. Our responses confirm gratitude that we are alive. Feeding ourselves from this premise is "communion" with life, generating love and gratitude with every meal.

To Life!

The care of the earth is our most ancient, most worthy and, after all our most pleasing responsibility. To cherish what remains of it and to foster its renewal is our only legitimate hope.

Wendell Berry

APPENDIX A

NVC Basics

"We can make life miserable or wonderful for ourselves and others depending upon how we think and communicate."

Marshall Rosenberg

Nonviolent Communication (NVC) is a language of compassion and offers a path to which we can return when we lose our way in the complexities of relationship. The integration of thinking, feeling, and intuition is at the heart of NVC training and the domain of the consciousness it cultivates. Practicing NVC grounds words and actions in a consciousness that cultivates compassionate connection with others by identifying the needs that underlie our own and others' feelings and actions. In this appendix are some of the basic forms and distinctions of NVC that Marshall Rosenberg (its founder) refers to as the map used to find the territory. The territory is the consciousness.

Thousands of years of cultural strategies based in domination and control are deeply embedded within our patterns of communication. NVC brilliantly identifies such patterns and offers life-enriching alternatives. Marshall Rosenberg's book, Nonviolent Communication: A Language of Life, is a quick, easy, and excellent read for those wanting to learn the basics. As with any art, these rudiments necessarily must be learned, practiced, understood, embodied, and then let go so as not to become rote and block creativity. Like training wheels on a bike, they help us learn, and at the same time, if depended upon too heavily, can eventually impede us.

NVC in its most expansive form is a way of life, and its principles of non-violence can be practiced anywhere. NVC is brilliant in its simplicity, with many distinctions and nuanced skills to learn. NVC skills emphasize taking personal responsibility for our feelings, actions, and the choices we make when we respond to others, as well as how to contribute to relationships based in cooperation and collaboration. With NVC, we train with the intention to connect on the heart level and, as much as possible, keep our attention in the present moment and not stuck in the past of the "he-said/she-said" blame and shame game.

Honesty and empathy are two of NVC's core skill building.

- **Honesty** in the form of expressing your present-moment observations, feelings, needs, and requests.

- **Empathy** in the form of connecting with another person's present-moment feelings and needs

Empathy begins with self-empathy in the form of connecting with your own present-moment feelings and needs (experiencing them internally beyond simply naming them). Empathy, self-empathy, and honesty are practiced and expressed through four components—observations, feelings, needs, and requests.

Observation: To state concrete, clear observations of actions you *observe* in yourself or the other person. It helps to describe observations as something that can be clearly captured on a video camera. Be sure to separate moral judgments and evaluations from the specific behaviors and conditions that are being observed. (This is much more difficult than it sounds.)

Feelings: State the *feeling* that the observation is triggering in you. Or, guess what the other person is feeling, and ask. Identify and articulate what you are feeling as distinguished from what you are thinking or the judgments you may have. Feelings include emotions, body sensations, moods, and states of mind.

Needs: Once you know what you are feeling, use that to help identify and articulate your needs. In NVC, "needs" are essential, universal human needs we all have in common, such as safety, belonging, and understanding. NVC practices distinguish needs from the strategies we use to meet our needs. If your perception of a need includes a specific person, place, action, time, or object, it is a strategy masquerading as a need.

Requests: Make *requests* that are clear, positive, actionable, and that honor one another's needs. Be sure to tell the other person what you would like them to *do*, never what you want them not to do, or what you want them to stop doing. The primary difference between a request and a demand is that, if the other person says "no" to your request, there are never any negative repercussions.

If you are feeling upset, instead of thinking about what's wrong with others or yourself, think about what need of yours is not being met and what could be done to meet it.

Mourning and Celebration: We mourn what we love that we miss and celebrate what is present in our lives that we love. Both forms of gratitude are essential to healing, and their expression honors life.

The Four D's are ways of thinking that disconnect us from ourselves and others:

- **Diagnosis** - judgment, blame, criticism, and labeling.
- **Denial** - of responsibility for our own feelings and actions, or denying someone else theirs.
- **Demand** - a form of coercion rather than request.
- **Deserve** - assuming that certain behaviors merit certain consequences—either reward or punishment.

Don't put your "but" in someone's face, especially if they are angry. Learn to replace the word "but" with "and" or "at the same time," which will help you rework the sentence into a more congruent and positive statement.

Sorry - Whenever you want to say you are sorry, instead of self-deprecating supplication, express your sadness and true regrets for what you have done and what you would have loved to have done instead. A different way of saying I am sorry might be: "I regret what I just said. It didn't meet my need to help us connect in ways that honor one another."

Exaggerations and Generalizations - Mixing what you actually observe with exaggerations and generalizations will invite conflict. Be careful using words like never, frequently, always, usually, a lot, many, seldom, etc. Practice being as clear and precise as possible with the words you use to describe what you observe.

"Should-ing" - "Should" is a socially acceptable yet veiled demand we make of others or ourselves. Whenever "should" is spoken, notice how it feels to receive, then translate it into a question to yourself as to whether it is something you will- ingly choose to do or not.

Reflecting - When things get emotional, ask if you can reflect what the other is saying because you really want to hear what they want you to understand. When someone experiences you doing your best to understand him or her, there is very little for them to resist.

Similarly, ask others to reflect back what you have said so you can make sure you have expressed yourself clearly. (When making this request, be careful to express it in a way that reflects concern about your own clarity and will not make the other person think you are accusing them of not listening.)

Demand or Request - When asking someone to do something, check first to see if you are making a request or if it is really a demand. Will you be upset if they say "no"? Then it's a demand, not a request. Wait until you feel differently to ask for help.

It's Hard to do a Don't - Instead of requesting what you don't want someone to do, say what you do want the person to do in clear, positive, doable language. Similarly, avoid telling another person what you want them to stop doing.

Find Common Ground - We can have empathy for another person without agreeing with their opinion or their decision (strategy). That is the common ground we all walk on—the ability to hear and value each other's feelings and needs, even when we don't agree.

Yes behind the No - Instead of saying "no," say what need of yours is preventing you from saying "yes."When another person tells you "no," remember they are saying "no" to your request, not to you, and that it's because they have a need that is preventing them from saying "yes" in that moment.

Expressing Gratitude - Instead of praising someone who did something you like, express your gratitude by telling the person what need of yours that action met.

Moral Judgments and Labeling - Whenever you use the words, "You are....," remember that you are either labeling or making a personal judgment of another. Instead, tell the other person what feelings their behavior stimulates in you and how it affects you.

Appreciation - We are often taught to use appreciation as a means of manipulation instead of a sincere celebration of how our lives have been enriched. Instead of giving compliments that are really judgments, we provide meaningful appreciation by telling other people how their actions have helped meet our needs. We can also request confirmation that we have contributed to another's well-being as a way of meeting our need for appreciation.

40 words - We can often lose connection by using more than 40 words at a time in any heated dialogue.

Beware of Labels - Move away from the use of static labels to analyze, criticize, or categorize. Practice speaking in ways that recognize and honor one another as changing beings.

Some Marshallisms

Here are some quotes Marshall Rosenberg shared in his trainings:

- "Every diagnosis is a self-fulfilling prophecy. What you see is who you get."
- "When you see someone as complaining, you are already in diagnosis. You have to learn how to enjoy their pain."
- "Empathic connection before fixing."
- "Only empathize if it is something you are doing for yourself. When it meets your need to go surfing with the divine energy. If not, then do something else."
- "When you want someone to change, consider both what it is that you'd like the other person to do differently and what do you want their reasons to be for doing it?"
- "When you're feeling positive, your needs are met."
- "When you're feeling negative, your needs are not met."
- "We all meet our needs to the best of our abilities."
- "Empathize, don't justify."
- "Unexpressed fear is almost always heard as aggression."
- "Rewards take the rewards out of it."
- "Respect as a feeling is a bit dangerous because we think we get it from another."
- "To give is domination if I cannot receive."
- "When someone is talking a lot, look for need under the pain that is moving him or her to talk."
- "When someone is talking a lot, you can say, 'I need you to stop, and I need to know what you want from me.' The feeling under the words must be patient.
- On regrets he said, "We do things we wouldn't have done if we knew then what we are learning now."
- "Do not think what you say is empathy; this is off target. Empathy is where we connect our consciousness with our intentions."
- "A hug is a mug when you give it to someone when they need empathy. When you do it to get rid of the pain because you can't stand their pain."
- "We are responsible for our intentions and actions."
- "How others reinterpret our actions and intentions is what creates their feelings. This is out of our control, and we cannot be responsible for their feelings."
- "When people keep repeating themselves is where they need empathy."

APPENDIX B

Needs and Feelings

A brilliant distinction that NVC brings forth is that our deeper individual and mutual needs are one and the same, and that where we experience conflict is in the strategies we choose to meet our needs. Identifying needs gives us both the focus and the energy to find the necessary words and take effective action—to form the kinds of requests that produce life-enriching results. Marshall Rosenberg and other trainers often give a list of words that help identify needs. Increasing our "needs and feelings" vocabulary to express such qualities of being is revelatory and essential, but words alone fall short in expressing the actual beauty and scope of what needs actually are. Universal human needs are something we all share, and the notion is that we all have an equal right to have our needs met. I extend this idea to include the nonhuman the world as well, recognizing our partnership and equality with the plants, animals, and earth as a whole. In other words, no one's spirit is greater or lesser. It is how we think, judge, and interpret that differs. When we focus primarily on our different ways of thinking, we can easily lose sight of our humanness and the deep needs that we all share.

NEEDS

CONNECTION

acceptance
affection
appreciation
belonging
cooperation
closeness
community
companionship
compassion
consideration
consistency
empathy
inclusion
intimacy
love
mutuality
nurturing
respect
self-respect
safety
security
stability
support
to know and be
  known
to see and be
  seen
to understand

and be understood
trust
warmth

PHYSICAL WELL-BEING

air
food
movement
exercise
rest/sleep
sexual expression
safety
shelter
touch water

HONESTY

authenticity
integrity
presence

PLAY

joy
humor

PEACE

beauty communion
ease equality
harmony
inspiration
order

AUTONOMY

choice freedom
independence space
spontaneity

MEANING

awareness
celebration of life
challenge
clarity
competence
consciousness
contribution
creativity
discovery
efficacy
effectiveness
growth
hope learning
mourning
participation
purpose
expression
stimulation to
matter
understanding

FEELINGS

Words describe experience. Most of us have a very limited vocabulary for how we feel. We feel good, okay, bad, tired, busy, or sad. Expanding our vocabulary and ability to feel into sensation and articulate the nuances of what we feel clarifies the messages we send. Thoughts convey to the listener what we are thinking. Feelings convey to the listener our emotional and/or physical states.

Generally, thoughts precede what we feel and what we feel can dominate our thoughts. Thoughts or beliefs (which are also thoughts) may be conscious or unconscious. Some of our core beliefs are buried deep below the surface of our awareness. A feeling can occur alone, and the mind will search for a thought, a story, to attach to it. That is precarious, because often the story isn't actually connected to the feeling; however, our mind likes to have an explanation. In order to be fully understood when discussing a conflict, the listener needs to know the speaker's thoughts and feelings. Therefore, feelings and thoughts need to be clearly differentiated and articulated. This all matters for one simple reason: thoughts and feelings are two different types of data. More data and accurate data gives us the best shot at being understood, loved, and respected. When we hear the word "I feel" followed by "like," "as if," or "that" and then a pronoun or a person's name, the statement is a thought, not a feeling. Let's explore this somatically:

1. First imagine you are speaking with someone. Now, with feeling, say each sentence below, one at a time, as if each were true for you. After each sentence, notice whether what you are actually feeling is actually clear to you or not.

ï   I feel *like* you do not understand me.

ï   It feels *as if* we are never going to be together.

ï   I feel *like* you don't care about a clean house.

ï   I feel *like* Bob is heading for some big problems.

2. Now we'll add a true feeling after the word "feel." Read this set of sentences and see if what you feel is clearer:

ï   I feel *frustrated* when you tell me you will be on time and then you arrive late.

ï   I feel *hopeless* trying to find the connection I so want with you.

ï   I feel *pissed* when I come home to such a mess.

ï   I feel *scared* when I see Bob drinking every night.

The first set of sentences each express a thought rather than a feeling. Receiving such statements will most likely be heard as evaluation or criticism. The second set of sentences conveys clearly the feeling experienced by the speaker. When our communication transmits that we are taking responsibility for our feelings, the listener will relax more and is less likely to hear blame or judgment.

A LIST OF FEELINGS WHEN YOUR NEEDS ARE SATISFIED

AFFECTIONATE
compassionate
friendly
loving
open hearted
sympathetic
tender
warm

ENGAGED
absorbed
alert curious
engrossed
enchanted
entranced
fascinated
interested
intrigued
involved
spellbound
stimulated

HOPEFUL
expectant
encouraged
optimistic

CONFIDENT
empowered
open
proud safe
secure

EXCITED
amazed
animated
ardent
aroused
astonished
dazzled eager
energetic
enthusiastic
giddy
invigorated
lively
passionate
surprised
vibrant

GRATEFUL
appreciative
moved

thankful
touched

INSPIRED
amazed
awed
wonder

JOYFUL
amused
delighted
glad happy
jubilant
pleased
tickled

EXHILARATED
blissful
ecstatic
elated
enthralled
exuberant
radiant
rapturous
thrilled

A LIST OF FEELINGS WHEN YOUR NEEDS ARE <u>NOT</u> SATISFIED

AFRAID

apprehensive

CONFUSED

ambivalent

EMBARRASSED

ashamed

TENSE

anxious dread

foreboding

frightened

mistrustful

panicked

petrified

scared

suspicious

terrified wary

worried

ANNOYED

aggravated

dismayed

disgruntled

displeased

exasperated

frustrated

impatient

irritated irked

ANGRY

enraged

furious

incensed

indignant

irate

livid

outraged

resentful

AVERSION

animosity

baffled

bewildered

dazed

hesitant lost

mystified

perplexed

puzzled torn

DISCONNECTED

alienated

aloof

apathetic

bored cold

detached

distant

distracted

indifferent

numb removed

uninterested

withdrawn

DISQUIET

agitated

alarmed

discombobulated

disconcerted

disturbed perturbed

rattled

restless

shocked

chagrined

flustered

guilty

mortified

self-conscious

FATIGUE

beat burnt

out

depleted

exhausted

lethargic

listless

sleepy

tired

A LIST OF FEELINGS WHEN YOUR NEEDS ARE <u>NOT</u> SATISFIED

weary
worn out

PAIN
agony
anguished
bereaved
devastated
grief
heartbroken
hurt
lonely
miserable
regretful
remorseful

SAD
depressed
dejected
despair
cranky
distressed
distraught
edgy fidgety
frazzled

irritable jittery
nervous
overwhelmed
restless stressed
out

VULNERABLE
fragile
guarded
helpless
insecure
leery
reserved
sensitive shaky

YEARNING
envious
jealous
longing
nostalgic
pining
wistful
appalled
contempt
disgusted

dislike
hate
horrified
hostile
repulsed
startled
surprised
troubled
turbulent
turmoil
uncomfortable
uneasy
unnerved
unsettled
despondent
disappointed
discouraged
disheartened
forlorn gloomy
heavy hearted
hopeless
melancholy
unhappy

RESOURCES

Buhner, S. (2004The Secret Teachings of Plants: The Intelligence of the Heart in the Direct Perception of Nature(Bear and Company)

Claire Silvia, Clare (1998) A Change of Heart, Mass Market Paperback

Conger, John P. The Body in Recovery: Somatic Psychotherapy and the Self by Frog Ltd., 1(994.

Chilton Pierce, Joseph (2002) The Anatomy of Transcendence (Park Street Press)

Chilton Pierce, Joseph (2010 The Heart-Mind Matrix: How the Heart Can Teach the Mind New Ways to Think Paperback

Eisler, R. (1988 The Chalice and the Blade: Our History, Our Future by (Harper SanFrancisco,

Gendlin, E. (1982) Focusing (Bantam Press)

Hanna, T. (1988 Somatics: Reawakening the Mind's Control of Movement, Flexibility, and Health. Cambridge, MA (HarperCollins Publishers, 1988)

Johnson, H.D. (1995 Bone, Breath, & Gesture: Practices of Embodiment. Berkeley, CA (North Atlantic Books)

Keleman, S. (1986 Emotional Anatomy: The Structure of Experience. Berkeley, CA (Center Press

Kurtz, R. (1990 Body-Centered Psychotherapy: The Hakomi Method: The Integrated Use of Mindfulness, Nonviolence and the Body (Life Rhythm)

Levine, P.A. & Frederick, A. (1997 Waking the Tiger: Healing Trauma: The Innate Capacity to Transform Overwhelming Experiences. Berkeley, Ca (North Atlantic Books)

Lowen, A. (1994) Bioenergetics. New York, NY (Penguin)

Macnaughton, I. (2004) Body, Breath, and Consciousness (North Atlantic Press)

Muller, W. (1993 Legacy of the Heart: The Spiritual Advantages of a Painful Childhood

Palmer, W. (1994 The Intuitive Body: Aikido as a Clairsentient Practice. Berkeley, CA (North Atlantic Books)

Rosenberg, M. (2003 Nonviolent Communication: A Language of Life, 2nd ed. Encinitas, CA

Saotome, M. (1993) The Harmony of Nature (Shambala Press)

Selznick, P. (1992 The Moral Commonwealth (University of California Press=

Strozzi-Heckler, R. (1993 The Anatomy of Change: A Way to Move Through Life's Transitions. Berkeley, CA (North Atlantic Books)

Strozzi-Heckler, R. (1997 Holding the Center: Sanctuary in a Time of Confusion. Berkeley, CA (Frog, Ltd.)

Claire Silvia, Clare (1998) A Change of Heart, Mass Market Paperback

Made in the USA
San Bernardino, CA
26 January 2018